Language Acquisition Program for the Retarded or Multiply Impaired

Louise R. Kent

Research Press
2612 N. Mattis Avenue · Champaign, Illinois 61820

ISBN 0-87822-121-2

Support received from
    Michigan Department of Mental Health
    Western Michigan University Faculty Research Fund
    Department of Health, Education and Welfare, Grant Number 51-p-70820-5-01

Fifth printing 1979

Formerly published as *Language Acquisition Program for the Severely Retarded*

to

WARREN L. TODD, III

Contents

Illustrations

Acknowledgments

In addition to the children, many people have contributed to the development of the LAP through its several revisions and through supporting research. Foremost among them have been Thomas Elzinga, Arthur Falk, Hartmut Guenther, Diane Klein, Marsha Williams, Karen Bunker, Stanley Winter, Tom Cross, and others too numerous to mention. The author wishes to gratefully acknowledge their thoughtful and enthusiastic assistance. Others who have maintained a continuing interest on a consulting level have been Fred Keller, Murray Sidman, Jack Michael, and James McLean.

Special thanks are due to Martha Snell and Erland W. Gleason for their chapters included in this volume; both have made a substantial contribution.

I also wish to gratefully acknowledge the tireless assistance of Dolores Eddy in typing the many drafts of previous unpublished versions of the program and in keeping the mailing list current and accurate. The sometimes seemingly insurmountable problems of distribution have been greatly facilitated through the cooperation of the Coldwater State Home and Training School and the Western Michigan University Child Development Center. Thanks go to all who have contributed in this effort.

And, finally, I gratefully acknowledge the cooperation of the officers of University Park Press, Baltimore, Md., publisher of *Language Intervention with the Retarded* edited by James E. McLean, David E. Yoder, and Richard L. Schiefelbusch, 1972, a volume which included the 1970 version of the LAP.

Overview and Procedures

PROGRAM OVERVIEW

The Language Acquisition Program (LAP) is designed to teach a language system to severely retarded children. Though structured primarily for oral administration with hearing, sighted, severely retarded children, it has also been used successfully with children diagnosed as visually handicapped, hearing handicapped, autistic, emotionally disturbed, aphasic or brain damaged.

The LAP has evolved over a period of eight years and synthesizes clinical experience, research results, principles of reinforcement theory, and principles of programmed instruction. Its content, sequencing of the content, and the procedures are carefully detailed to insure each child's success as a learner. The program is not perfectly sequenced. Unanticipated difficulties are to be expected in its administration. The program should be modified if a child does not respond to this sequence. It is partly on this basis that the program has acquired its present form.

The content of the program consists of a variety of tasks which are sequenced according to presumed difficulty. The sequence for any particular child, however, is partially individualized; i.e., the child's performance affords him certain options and disallows others. Administration of the program requires the presentation of content be taught in the prescribed manner coupled with the immediate reinforcement of the child's correct or near-correct responses.

The program is divided into three major sections: Pre-Verbal, Verbal-Receptive, and Verbal-Expressive. The Pre-Verbal Section stresses the acquisition of prerequisite attending behaviors and motor imitation. The verbal sections introduce the acquisition of selected receptive and expressive language skills. Each section is divided into phases; each phase is divided into parts. The Table of Contents describes the system used to identify the phases and parts of the sections. The recommended sequence through the program is described in Figure 1 and also in Chapter 4.

The language system may be predominantly oral, predominantly manual, or some combination of the two. Ordinarily, the trainer begins by using an oral approach. But there are several reasons that he might choose a manual language approach:

1. The child is known to be deaf or hard of hearing and has not responded adequately to oral training.

2. The child is known to be deaf or hard of hearing, gives some positive response to oral training, but due to his advanced age needs a functional language system as quickly as possible.

3. The child, for unknown reasons, has not responded adequately to the expressive aspects of oral training.

The LAP has been adapted to deaf sign by Martha Snell in Chapter 6.

If the trainer wishes to evaluate the child's performance to determine his entry point into the program, he can use the Inventory in Chapter 5 which was developed by Erland W. Gleason. However, no harm is done if the trainer starts at the beginning for every child. What is critical is that the child experiences a high density of success from the very first day. The Inventory can also be used as an assessment instrument at various intervals within the program to get an independent check on the child's development.

Figure 1   Sequence of Phases in Verbal Sections*

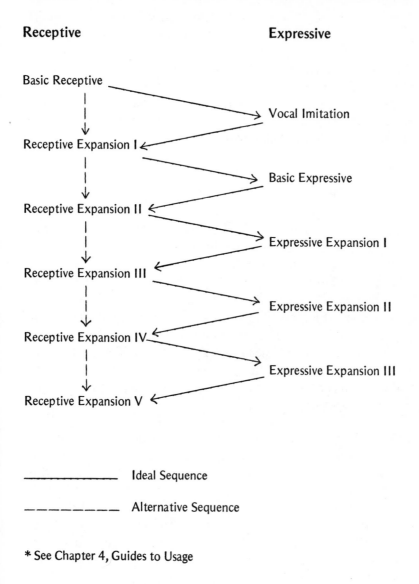

Receptive   **Expressive**

Basic Receptive → Vocal Imitation

Receptive Expansion I → Basic Expressive

Receptive Expansion II → Expressive Expansion I

Receptive Expansion III → Expressive Expansion II

Receptive Expansion IV → Expressive Expansion III

Receptive Expansion V

——————— Ideal Sequence

——————— Alternative Sequence

* See Chapter 4, Guides to Usage

BASIC PROCEDURES

The training procedures that are more or less standard throughout the program are based on the principles of reinforcement theory.* Central to the theory is the principle of positive reinforcement which states that the likelihood of reoccurrence of a behavior will be increased if that particular behavior is immediately reinforced when it first occurs. Application of this principle enables the teacher or trainer to strengthen a desirable behavior by reinforcing it whenever it occurs. Successful application of the principle requires that desirable behaviors be reinforced immediately.

Tokens

Usually the trainer will find that verbal praise paired with consumables (bites of ice cream, M&Ms, Cheezos, potato chips, sugar-coated cereals, crushed ice, sips of Kool-Aid, etc.) are initially the most effective reinforcers; however, the trainer should not hesitate to employ anything else that might serve as an effective reinforcer for a particular child. The reinforcer should always be accompanied by verbal praise such as *Good,* or *Good job,* since it is possible to deliver such social reinforcers more quickly than edibles can be consumed. The social reinforcer serves to bridge the gap between the response and the edible reinforcer and may, in time, become effective without the support of edibles.

In many cases the trainer will want to establish a token system in which tokens, such as checkers or play money, are used as substitutes for edibles. Tokens are much more convenient to use during training than are edibles. They can easily be delivered immediately after correct responses, and their delivery does not usually interrupt the ongoing behavior. Furthermore, the child can be allowed to exchange them for a wide variety of reinforcers at the end of the training session. In

---

* Fred S. Keller, *Learning: Reinforcement theory* (New York: Random House, 1969).

this way he is not likely to become satiated on a particular type of reinforcer. There are many effective ways to implement a token system.

When the child makes a correct response, he is given verbal praise, an edible, and a token such as a checker. The checker is placed on a spindle. The presentation of each token is always paired with enthusiastic verbal praise. When the spindle is full, the child is allowed to exchange his tokens for his choice from an array of goods or edibles. The child quickly learns that the tokens have redemption value; the use of edibles along with tokens for each correct response can usually be eliminated within one session.

The child is now receiving a token and verbal praise for each correct response; a token exchange takes place each time that the spindle is full. This procedure quickly gives way to an intermediate exchange; for example, when the spindle is full, the child receives a colored chain link in exchange for his tokens. At the end of the session, or after about 30 minutes, the connected chain of links is exchanged for the available goods or edibles.

The use of the spindle allows the child to gain some visual awareness of numbers, and occasions the acquisition of the concept of something being "full."

In the expressive phases of the program, the child is required to request by name the reinforcer in response to *What do you want?* Any reasonable approximation is acceptable. The child is also expected to respond appropriately when the trainer asks *Who has tokens?* The child is prompted to respond with some approximation of *Me* or *I do.* The token exchange situation, regardless of phase, provides an appropriate setting for the trainer to prompt the responses *More* and *All gone. Do you want more juice? Say, More. Have you finished your juice?* Point to the bottom of the empty cup and say *Your juice is all gone. Say, All gone.* These responses are recorded on the bottom of the LAP Data Sheet(s) in the space provided for Token Exchange Behavior (see Figure 2).

Further description of the verbal aspects of the token exchange is provided in 3.20 Basic Expressive Phase.

5

Figure 2   Data Sheet

Child's name _____   Date _____

Trainer's name _____   Session number _____

Trial	1	2	3	4	5	6	7	8	9	10
1										
2										
3										
4										
5										
6										
7										
8										
9										
10										
11										
12										
13										
14										
15										
16										
17										
18										
19										
20										
21										
22										
23										
24										
No.										
C										
A										
I										
NR										

Token Exchange Behavior

Phase _____

Part _____

No. Sessions completed on part

_____

Check One:

I-I _____

Training session

    Test-step _____

    Teach-step _____

F-I _____

Retention Check _____

Data Summary Totals

No. Trials presented _____ (a)

No. Correct R's _____ (b)

No. Approximations_____

No. Incorrect R's _____

No. NR's _____

% Correct _____

$$\left(\frac{b}{a} \times 100\right)$$

_____

_____

Extraneous Responses Response	Comment

Initial Inventory

Prior to the administration of training sessions on any part in the program the trainer administers the Initial Inventory (I-I) for that part. The I-I consists of a randomized sequence of each behavior to be learned in that part (usually two trials on each). The child's performance in the I-I guides the trainer in deciding the order for teaching the behaviors in that part. The behaviors which the child approximates in the I-I will presumably be easier to learn than those which he performs incorrectly or not at all. **The presumed easier-to-learn behaviors are always taught first.**

Test and Teach

Each training session consists of a Test- and a Teach-step. The trainer first presents a review or test of all behaviors which were performed correctly in the I-I as well as those which the child has learned in training sessions (two trials on each previously learned item); the order of presentation of items should be random. The trainer begins a trial only when the child is exhibiting appropriate attending behavior, including pre-trial eye contact. All correct responses are immediately reinforced with verbal praise and either tokens or consumable reinforcers. Although responses may be prompted in the Test-step, prompted responses are not counted as correct. If criterion is met on the test, including all items previously correct, the trainer trains a new behavior in the Teach-step. If criterion is not met on the test, any item(s) failed is retaught to criterion in the Teach-step before any new item is introduced. **Old items are always retaught before new ones are introduced.**

When the trainer introduces a new behavior, the child will usually only approximate the desired behavior, or he will emit the behavior only if the trainer provides prompts, an imitative model, or physical assistance. During the Teach-step, the trainer reinforces all correct responses; he also reinforces appropriate responses made after the child has been prompted, provided with an imitative model, or physically assisted in performing the task.

It is not necessary to use such language as *No,* or *Let's try again,* or *That's not quite right,* all of which connotes failure or inadequate performance. When a child fails to respond to the verbal command, the trainer repeats the command and supplies the least amount of help needed for the child to make the desired response. "Help" may consist of (1) a prompt which may be uttered or gestured, (2) an imitative model by which the trainer shows the child exactly how to respond, or (3) physical assistance; i.e., the trainer physically assists the child in making the response. The trainer tries to gradually withdraw physical assistance, imitative models, and prompts (in that order). Thus, the child gradually learns to make correct responses to the verbal instructions alone. The strategy of gradually withdrawing help is sometimes called "fading." It enables the child to learn without failure. **A training trial should always end with success.**

Specifically, new items are introduced by the following steps:

1. The trainer presents the new item via the appropriate verbal command. If the child responds correctly, he proceeds to Step 2. If the child responds incorrectly or does not respond, the trainer again presents the command and provides a prompt, a model, or physical assistance as needed. This procedure is followed until the child responds correctly on two consecutive trials to the verbal command alone. The trainer should present no more than approximately 20 trials on the same item in any one session and never more than two **consecutive** trials on the same item. If the item being taught is the only one in the child's repertoire in that part, the trainer must alternate trials on it with trials on some response that is in the child's repertoire. **It is extremely important to surround trials on new items with trials on already mastered ones.**

2. After two consecutive correct responses on the new item have been obtained, the trainer alternates the item with the first response taught or a response

which was scored as correct in the I-I. If an error is made on either item, the trainer returns to Step 1 and then back to Step 2.

3. When two correct responses on the new item have been obtained in Step 2, the trainer introduces another item in the part **or** alternates it with **two** items that are already in the child's repertoire. The trainer continues this procedure, gradually introducing items and then mixing them with more and more previously mastered items, until the child responds correctly on all of them in a random sequence. If an error is made on any item in Step 3, the trainer backs up to Step 2, alternating the missed item with only one correct item, rather than two or more. If an error is again made on the same item, the trainer goes back to Step 1. If an error is made on a previously taught item in the Test-step in any session, he employs the principle: **Old items are always retaught before new ones are introduced.**

Final Inventory and Retention Check
When the child appears to have learned all of the behaviors in a part, the trainer administers a Final Inventory (F-I), including each of the behaviors in the part, and presents each behavior two times in a random order. If final criterion is met, the trainer then administers the F-I on all previously completed parts of the phase. This is the Retention Check. If criterion is not met, training is resumed until administration of another F-I is indicated or until 10 sessions are completed.

In the Verbal Sections, no more than 10 consecutive sessions are administered on any one part. This is the **10-Session Rule.** If criterion is not met by the tenth session on a part, training on that part is temporarily suspended. When training is resumed, the trainer begins again by administering an I-I on the discontinued part. The 10-Session Rule applies only to the Verbal Sections.

After 10 training sessions on any part, the trainer administers a Retention Check on all parts previously completed in the phase. If retention is 90%, the child proceeds to a new part, resumes training on a previously discontinued part, or enters a new phase if indicated. If retention is less than criterion, the trainer must retrain to criterion the part(s) in question before proceeding to a new part or phase.

Criterion

Each part has a criterion which must be met by the child before moving further through the program. Though criterion varies with each part, standard criterion predominates. Criterion is standard when 90% of the responses are correct on a random sequence, including all items, two trials on each. The two trials on the same items are not necessarily successive.

Some parts of the program include non-criterion tasks in addition to the basic tasks. Criterion on a part is based entirely upon performance of the basic tasks. The non-criterion tasks are included to facilitate generalization and retention and to introduce later content; mastery is not required. In each part the basic task is taught first to criterion. If criterion is reached before the tenth session, the non-criterion tasks are introduced. Once the non-criterion tasks are introduced, each training session on the part must include a criterion performance on the basic task. Provided criterion is met on the basic task, training on the non-criterion tasks may begin. Again, no more than 10 consecutive sessions are administered on any one part. For example, if criterion on a part is met by the end of the sixth session, the non-criterion tasks may be used for the remaining four sessions provided the child maintains his criterion performance on the basic task.

Retention Checks: The non-criterion tasks need not be included since criterion is based entirely on the basic task. If retraining on the basic task is indicated, training on the non-criterion tasks should be discontinued until criterion is again met on the basic task. The 10-Session Rule still applies.

Pre-Session Preparation

Before any session begins, the trainer should know what he is going to do with the child and have on hand the needed teaching materials, reinforcers, and data sheets. The data sheets that the trainer expects to use are prepared in advance with identifying information and, to a certain extent, with the content of the session, before the child enters the training situation. A data sheet is presented in Figure 3.

The key word of the item or desired behavior should be filled in along the horizontal axis at the top of the grid. Although items are presented to the child in a random order in the Teach- and Test-steps, for any given child the items should appear on the data sheets in a fixed order in all training sessions on any particular part; the most recently added item appears last (to the right at the top of the horizontal axis). The first items to appear on the horizontal axis will be those that were correct on the I-I, or those on which training was initiated. When preparing the data sheet for a training session, the trainer should pre-determine and note on the data sheet the next item to be presented, regardless of whether the item actually is presented during that session.

Data Recording

A trial consists of the trainer giving the command for the task and the child's response. Each time the trainer presents a trial the child's response is recorded in the square corresponding to the trial number and the command. (Note that for any one session many squares remain blank; **this is correct**.) The following symbols are used in recording the child's responses:

Correct response	✓
Approximation	⊘
Incorrect response	✕
No response	◯

The data for each item are tallied at the bottom of the grid and summarized in the space provided.

Figure 3   Sample Data Sheet

Child's name __S. Kiener__   Date __10-15-74__

Trainer's name __F. Moore__   Session number __32__

Trial	box 1	Table 2	door 3	light 4	chair 5	6	7	8	9	10
1	✓									
2		✓								
3			✓							
4		✓								
5				✓						
6	✓									
7		✓								
8			✓							
9		✓								
10				✓						
11	✓									
12			✓							
13					◯					
14					⊘					
15				✓						
16					✕					
17		✓								
18					◯					
19		✓								
20					⊘					
21					⊘					
22	✓									
23		✓								
24					⊘					
No. C	4	7	3	3	0					
A					4					
I					1					
NR					2					

Phase __3.2.0__

Part __3.2.3 (room parts)__

No. Sessions completed on part

            __6__

Check One:

I-I _____

Training session

    Test-step _____

    Teach-step ____✓____

F-I _____

Retention Check _____

Data Summary Totals

No. Trials presented __24__ (a)

No. Correct R's __17__ (b)

No. Approximations __4__

No. Incorrect R's __1__

No. NR's __2__

% Correct __70%__

    ($\frac{b}{a}$ × 100)

Token Exchange Behavior

Rejected juice; pushed away + shook head. Imitated "No" easily — Spontaneously tried to count tokens today; /wʌ/, /u/, /i/ for all the rest.

Extraneous Responses

Response	Comment
light "bö" 2 times	for broken-bulb burned out.
C'mere Mo	for "Come here, Moore, trying to get me to follow him.
Oh, No!	First time I said "What is this?" re the chair.

As the child moves through the program his **extraneous** or unprogrammed verbal responses should be recorded. Some classes of extraneous responses should be reinforced and others should be ignored. For example, meaningless noises or babblings which appear to serve no useful function and which occur inappropriately should not be reinforced unless vocalizations of any kind do not occur; if this happens, the trainer should attempt to bring the babblings under appropriate imitative control.

Vocalizations unrecognizable as words or approximations to words, but which seem appropriate to the situation, should be reinforced if the child has no expressive repertoire and if appropriate vocalizations are rare. However, if the child can make some appropriate verbal responses and can also imitate, the trainer might choose to ignore the unrecognizable vocalizations or give the child a more appropriate response to imitate. Should the vocalization be stereotyped (same response regardless of item), the trainer should not reinforce it. (See 3.10 Vocal Imitation.)

The trainer will probably wish to reinforce responses which echo something that he has just uttered if the child has just started to imitate; the possibility of extinction of vocal imitation cannot be risked. On the other hand, the trainer does not want to shape indiscriminate imitation resembling echolalia. The child must eventually learn that he is to respond with vocal imitation only in the presence of the cue *Say* _____. Imitative extraneous responses are especially important to record and to describe in detail because they may assist the trainer in making decisions in subsequent session planning. If the child imitates "ball" in the Basic Receptive Phase, ball might well be the first item taught in the Basic Expressive Phase.

If the child inappropriately repeats or imitates what the trainer says, the child is exhibiting echolalia, for example:

Trainer: *Show me the shoe.*

Child: *Show me the shoe.*

It can be ignored in the receptive phases; however, in the expressive phases it must be dealt with directly as an interfering behavior. (See 3.10 Vocal Imitation.)

Verbalizations which may or may not be specifically related to the task at hand but are nevertheless appropriate should be reinforced unless they become excessive. The child might say something about the training materials; on the other hand, he might turn around and say *Hi, Mamma!* when another person enters the room. Either would be considered verbalizations under appropriate stimulus control; i.e., it is clear to the trainer what sorts of stimuli evoked the response. All verbalizations that seem to be under appropriate stimulus control should be reinforced and recorded until the recording becomes excessive. These responses can be useful to the trainer in making decisions about the content of later sessions.

Verbalizations which are excessive in frequency, appropriate or inappropriate, should be ignored. After each instance the trainer looks away and remains motionless for about 30 seconds. During this time the child is unable to earn tokens or to obtain social reinforcement. When the child remains still for at least 30 seconds, the trainer resumes the training activity.

The extraneous responses are recorded at the bottom of the LAP Data Sheet. There is a space for recording the response and a space for recording comments adjacent to it; comments might include anything relevant to the response which the trainer deems potentially useful to him.

Group Administration

The LAP is designed for individual administration. One trainer can work productively with two children at a time provided that both children remain seated with no problem. Although it is easier for the trainer, the two children need not be working on exactly the same parts. The trainer sits on one side of a square table. One child is seated on the trainer's left and one on his right; i.e., the children sit facing each other across the table. The trainer alternates trials between the two children. Whenever one child earns a token, the other child also receives a token provided he is attending appropriately. This procedure sets the stage for the observing child to learn from the other child, to learn to reinforce another child, and to learn to share the attention of the trainer.

A trainer cannot productively work with more than two children at a time on the LAP. Generally, two children will learn more in 30 minutes than four children in one hour.

1.00

Pre-Verbal Section

1.10 ATTENDING PHASE

This phase is designed to teach the child to sit quietly relaxed with his hands in his lap, to look wherever the trainer directs, and to look at the trainer prior to the presentation of any command. These attending behaviors are prerequisites for learning. It is important, therefore, that the trainer spend whatever time is necessary to complete this phase; time well spent here will pay off richly in ease of training in later parts of the program. If attending behaviors "slip" from control at any time, the trainer should take the time to bring them back under control before proceeding. **Nothing is more important to learning than good attending behavior.**

The content of this phase is not intrinsically interesting to the trainer or to the child. Reinforcers must be strong, such as ice cream. The reinforcement density must be high; consumable reinforcers should be paired with lots of enthusiastic praise.

1.11 Sitting Still

Initial Inventory. The trainer brings the child into the room, seats him in a chair, and places the child's hands in his lap. The trainer sits facing the child. If the child remains seated for 30 seconds, he meets criterion on this part so no training is required here. If the child leaves his seat before 30 seconds has elapsed, the trainer teaches the behavior.

Training. The trainer places the child in the chair and immediately reinforces him, usually with an edible, delaying delivery of reinforcers for increasingly longer intervals of sitting. Initially it may be necessary to restrain the child in the chair by sitting in front of him with the child's knees locked between the trainer's knees. The teaching procedure is continued until the child sits quietly with his hands in his lap for 30 seconds without physical restraint or prompting before being reinforced. If during any trial (in this instance, a trial is a prescribed time interval) the child leaves his seat, reseat him and, if necessary, back up to the reinforcement delay period of the previous trial.

Final Inventory. Final criterion is met when the child sits quietly relaxed with his hands in his lap for 30 seconds before being reinforced.

1.12 Elimination of Interfering Behaviors

Some children exhibit stereotyped behavior patterns such as weaving the head from side to side, rocking the shoulders back and forth, gazing at the hands, moving the fingers in various stereotyped ways. These behaviors interfere with "sitting still" as well as with all other forms of attending. If a child is unable to meet criterion on "sitting still" (as defined above) because of the presence of any of these types of self-stimulatory interfering behaviors, the "reversal procedure," which has been adapted from Azrin, Kaplan and Foxx,* is suggested.

* N. H. Azrin, S. J. Kaplan, and R. M. Foxx. Autism reversal: Eliminating stereotyped self-stimulation of retarded individuals. *American Journal of Mental Deficiency,* 1973, *78,* 3, 241-248.

The trainer exposes the child to several simple tasks such as stacking washers on a spindle, placing pegs in a pegboard, or dropping washers through a slot in the lid of a can. The trainer demonstrates the task to the child and then encourages him to perform it. After the child has had the opportunity to perform several different tasks, the trainer determines which task the child seems to enjoy most.

Once the trainer decides on the preferred task, he reinforces the child for performing it. The reinforcer should be an edible of high value to the child; i.e., miniature marshmallows, fruit loops, chocolate chips, bites of ice cream, sips of coke or whatever the child likes most. The edible reinforcer is accompanied with lavish social reinforcement such as smiles, hugs, and praise. The trainer reinforces the child after each appropriate response; for example, after each washer is stacked on the spindle. Very quickly, however, the trainer reinforces less frequently; i.e., he reinforces every other response, then every third, fifth, eighth, etc. The trainer then continues to reinforce the child's performance at least once every 60 seconds.

This training continues for at least eight sessions, conducted on different days. The trainer may utilize more than one task in a given session; the session length is extended gradually up to a minimum of 30 minutes for each child. During this time the child learns that when he attends to and performs the task the trainer is pleased with him and gives him a tasty edible. He also learns that receipt of warm praise and something good to eat is contingent upon his continuing to work.

The trainer then begins to respond differentially to the interfering behavior(s) when it occurs. He sets the child to task and reinforces continuous task performance every 60 seconds as before. If the child at any time begins to engage in the interfering behavior, he is immediately reprimanded by the trainer; e.g., *No, Tom, don't move your hands like that,* and is required to sit in another area of the room. The trainer then stands behind the child and requires him to engage in the appropriate reversal procedure (see below) for 20 minutes. At the end of 20 minutes, the child is returned to task and is reinforced for task performance as soon as it is performed and every 60 seconds thereafter. The total session length may vary depending on trainer time available; the trainer should plan on a minimum of one hour per child.

Whenever the child has engaged in less than 2 self-stimulatory episodes during the previous day, the duration of the reversal procedure is reduced from 20 minutes to 10 minutes, to 5 minutes, to 2 minutes, and then to a simple warning on successive days (the warning statement is the same as the original verbal reprimand). If exactly two episodes occur on a particular day, the duration is not changed for the next day. If more than 2 occur, the duration is increased back to the full 20 minutes on that day and on the following day. Once the procedure has been reduced to a simple warning, the child is given the warning for the first episode of the day and 2 minutes of the reversal procedure for the second episode that day.

When the child has exhibited no instances of the interfering behavior for two consecutive training sessions, the trainer proceeds to 1.13 Looking at Objects. In all subsequent sessions the child is given the warning for the first episode of the day and 2 minutes of reversal procedure for the second episode that day. If more than 2 episodes occur, the duration is increased back to the full 20 minutes on that day and on the following day.

Azrin, Kaplan, and Foxx (1973) have developed reversal procedures that are specific to the nature of the self-stimulatory behavior. The purpose of the reversal procedure is to eliminate interfering self-stimulatory behaviors. The form of a particular reversal procedure depends on the form of the particular interfering behavior to be eliminated. The same body parts are used in the reversal procedure as are involved in the interfering behavior; however, the movements used in the reversal procedure are incompatible with the performance of the interfering behavior. The rationale of the reversal procedure is to require guided practice in the performance of repeated postural changes that are incompatible with the performance of the interfering self-stimulatory behavior. Figure 4 illustrates the most common self-stimulatory behaviors and the reversal postures used for each.

Figure 4   Reversal Procedures for Self-Stimulatory Behavior

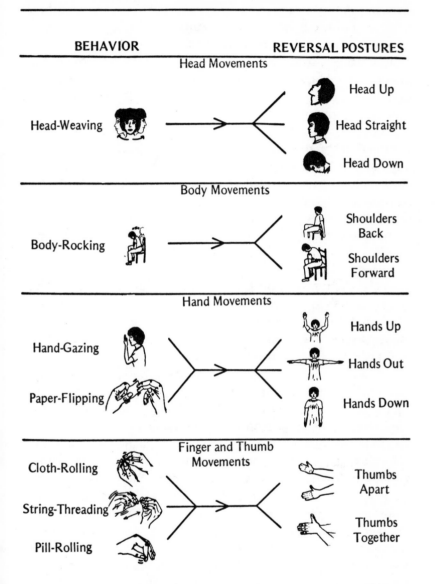

BEHAVIOR

REVERSAL POSTURES

Head Movements

Head-Weaving

Head Up

Head Straight

Head Down

Body Movements

Body-Rocking

Shoulders Back

Shoulders Forward

Hand Movements

Hand-Gazing

Paper-Flipping

Hands Up

Hands Out

Hands Down

Finger and Thumb Movements

Cloth-Rolling

String-Threading

Pill-Rolling

Thumbs Apart

Thumbs Together

Adapted from N. H. Azrin, S. J. Kaplan, and R. M. Foxx. Autism reversal: Eliminating stereotyped self-stimulation of retarded individuals. *American Journal of Mental Deficiency*, 1973, *78*, 3, 241-248.

Children who engage in "head-weaving" are required by instructions and manual guidance to maintain their heads in each of three postures: the head held upward, the head held straight, and the head held downward. Children who rock their bodies are required to practice maintaining their shoulders in two postures: shoulders forward away from the chair and shoulders back against the chair as in a normal sitting position. Children who engage in hand movements such as hand-gazing and paper-flipping are required to maintain their hands in each of three postures: hands extended above the head, hands outstretched from the sides of the body, and hands held to the sides of the body. Finger and thumb movements consisting of cloth-rolling, string-threading and pill-rolling are followed immediately by required practice in sustaining two postures: either the hands held together or the hands held apart. The children are required to maintain their thumbs in an upright position away from their fingers at approximately a 90° angle in both positions.

At the start of the reversal procedure the trainer gives the child the appropriate postural instruction (e.g., *head up, hands out,* or *shoulders back*). Talking to the child during the reversal procedure is limited to informative statements regarding the postures. Once a postural instruction has been given, the trainer waits approximately one second for the child to comply. Noncompliance results in the trainer quickly and manually guiding the child to the desired posture. If the child partially complies, the trainer applies only enough guidance for the child to complete the desired movement. Full compliance results in the trainer's following or "shadowing" the child's movement with a light touch of his hands. The trainer continues to shadow the child while he maintains each posture; the child is required to maintain each posture for 30 seconds. If resistance occurs while a posture is being maintained, the child is required to remain in that posture for 30 seconds with no resistance. When the reversal procedures involve three postures, the trainer varies the sequence in which the postural instructions are given; for those procedures involving two postures the trainer gives the instructions in simple alternation.

1.13 Looking at Objects

Initial Inventory. The trainer places five objects widely spaced on the table and points to one of the objects saying *Look at this.* The trainer does this for each of the five objects (five separate trials) in a random sequence and records whether the child looks at each as directed. If the child does not look as directed, the trainer must teach Looking at Objects. Choose objects which are used in 2.12.

Training. The trainer places one object on the table and points to it saying *Look at this.* If the child looks at the object, he is reinforced. If the child does not respond or responds incorrectly, the trainer may use physical assistance, such as turning the child's head toward the object, or a prompt, such as moving the object close to the child's face. If such strategies are not effective, it may be necessary for the trainer to use small dishes containing edibles rather than the objects. The trainer moves a small dish containing a few edibles close to the child's face and says *Look.* The trainer may tip the dish slightly toward the child at first. If the child looks into the dish, the trainer immediately reinforces him with an edible from the dish. The trainer then places the dish on the table and points to it saying *Look at this.* If the child does not respond or responds incorrectly, the trainer uses prompting procedures or physical assistance. Once the child looks at one dish on the table, the trainer introduces a second and a third dish spaced about the table and then teaches the child to look at them. This procedure is continued until the child looks at each dish correctly two times on command in a random sequence. The trainer then begins to substitute objects for the dishes of edibles. The objects are introduced one at a time until all three dishes have been replaced with objects. The trainer then proceeds to introduce a fourth and finally a fifth object.

Final Inventory. Final criterion is met when the child looks at each of five objects correctly on command in five random, consecutive trials.

1.14 Pre-Trial Eye Contact

Initial Inventory. The trainer places five objects on the table and directs the child to look at each by pointing and saying *Look at this.* The trainer does not record whether the child looks at the object as in part 1.13 Looking at Objects. Rather, he delays the presentation of each trial slightly and records whether the child looks, without prompts or physical assistance, at him prior to the presentation of each of the five *Look-at-this* trials. If the child does not look at the trainer prior to each trial, the trainer must then teach pre-trial eye contact.

Training. The trainer places the five objects on the table. Prior to each trial, he says *Look at me,* and waits. If the child looks at the trainer, the trainer immediately says *Look at this,* and points to one of the objects. If the child looks at the object, he is immediately reinforced. In a sense, the trainer uses the presentation of a *Look-at-this* trial as a reinforcer for pre-trial eye contact. When the child looks at the trainer on command prior to looking at the object on two consecutive trials, the trainer begins to delay the command *Look at me* for a few seconds, waiting for the child to look at him without the command. This procedure is continued until the child looks at the trainer without a command prior to the presentation of each *Look-at-this* trial for five consecutive trials. Commanding the child to *Look at me* should be faded out completely.

Sometimes it is extremely difficult to train the child to respond to *Look at me.* In some instances, it is helpful to call the child by name prior to saying *Look at me.* Be aware, however, of the tendency to depend on calling the child by name in order to maintain attending behavior. This is to be avoided. If the trainer is not careful, he will be reinforcing poor attending behavior with attention; and he will be wasting time nagging the child to look at him.

Final Inventory. Final criterion is met when the child makes eye contact with the trainer prior to the presentation of each of five *Look-at-this* trials without prompts.

Once the child has met criterion on the Attending Phase, he is ready to begin training in the Motor Imitation Phase. Attending behaviors must be maintained: if they slip, re-train.

1.20   MOTOR IMITATION PHASE

The ability to make specific motor responses, such as pointing, is a prerequisite for successful performance in later phases of the program. Therefore, those motor responses that are required of the child repeatedly throughout the program are taught, if necessary. Be aware that what is being taught are specific imitative responses deemed prerequisites for successful performance in later phases of this program; i.e., a generalized imitative repertoire is not the immediate objective.

1.21   Specific Motor Imitation

Initial Inventory. All imitative behaviors to be learned in this part are presented in the Initial Inventory. In a random sequence, including two trials on each item, the trainer presents the following behavioral models to the child accompanied by the command *Do this*.

The trainer points to an object on the table, one finger.

The trainer extends both hands in front of him.

The trainer points to his eyes, one with each forefinger.

The trainer points to his nose, one finger.

The trainer taps on his upper front teeth, one finger.

The trainer places one hand lightly on the top of his head, palm down.

The trainer points to his ears, one with each forefinger.

The trainer stands up.

The trainer sits down.

The trainer points to the ceiling light, one finger.

Those behaviors which are performed correctly in the I-I are included in all Test-steps in this part. Those behaviors which are not initially in the child's repertoire must be taught in the Teach-steps.

Training. The following is an example of a **training session** on Specific Motor Imitation.

Test-step. The trainer randomly presents those behaviors (two trials on each) that the child has already imitated correctly. If the child's responses are 90% correct on the randomized test, the trainer teaches the child a new imitative behavior.

Teach-step. The trainer presents the new behavior to be imitated preceded by the command *Do this.* For example, the trainer may say *Do this,* and point to an object on the table. If the child responds correctly by pointing to the object, he is reinforced. If the child does not respond or responds incorrectly, the trainer may use physical assistance, such as guiding the child's hand toward the object, after which the child is immediately reinforced. The trainer continues to reinforce successive approximations to the desired imitative response, gradually withdrawing physical assistance and gestural prompts until he imitates without help the trainer's pointing to the object. Training trials on the new behavior are interspersed with trials on behaviors already learned. When the child reaches standard criterion, a new behavior to be imitated may be added.

Final Inventory. Final criterion is standard on 20 trials of the 10 behaviors. Once final criterion is met, the child enters the Basic Receptive Phase.

For most children this procedure is satisfactory; criterion is met in a reasonable length of time. If a child appears to experience extreme difficulty, the trainer should consider two alternatives:

1. Alter the behaviors to be imitated. Tasks which involve simple object manipulation seem to be the easiest to imitate; for example, dropping a block in a can or pushing a car. The trainer should be certain that separate materials are available to the child and to him. If the child learns to imitate these kinds of tasks, the trainer begins to intersperse tasks which involve movements which are visible to the child as he performs them; for example, clapping hands, stomping feet, or extending both arms out to the front. It is easier to imitate movements that are visible than it is to imitate those that are not; and it is easier to imitate an action involving both arms or both feet than one which involves just one. By modifying the initial behaviors to be imitated in accordance with these suggestions and by gradually introducing new tasks interspersed with already mastered tasks, the trainer may ultimately be able to teach the tasks specified in 1.21 Specific Motor Imitation.

2. The trainer may proceed to the Basic Receptive Phase. However, 2.11 Pointing to Body Parts Named may need to be modified along the lines described in Step 1 above.

2.00

Verbal Section–Receptive

2.10   BASIC RECEPTIVE PHASE

The child may enter the Verbal Section—Receptive as soon as he meets final criterion on the Motor Imitation Phase. He enters via 2.10 Basic Receptive Phase. The purpose of the Basic Receptive Phase is to teach a limited receptive vocabulary. The child is required to respond differentially by pointing to or finding various objects, body parts, and room parts.

The trainer should administer the I-I's for 2.11, 2.12, and 2.13 before initiating training in this phase. All three options are available. In this first phase of the Verbal Section, however, only one part should be introduced at a time. The part on which I-I performance is best should be the first one entered.

As the child begins any part, an I-I is administered. Those behaviors which are already in the child's repertoire are included in all Test-steps for that part. Those behaviors which are not in the child's initial repertoire are taught in the training sessions using the Test-Teach procedure outlined in the Basic Procedures. When all behaviors of a particular part have been learned, a F-I is administered.

2.11   Pointing to Body Parts Named

In this part the child is required to point to and to touch (with the exception of "hands") the parts of his body named by the trainer. For example, *Show me Tommy's nose.* (Use the child's own name, initially.) The body parts are: ear, eye, hair, hand, nose, teeth. The first training session would include all items correct on the I-I plus one new item. For each item included in any session, the trainer first gives the verbal command. If the child responds appropriately, he is reinforced. If the child responds incorrectly or not at all, the trainer provides the imitative model accompanied by *Do this.* After the child makes a correct imitative response, the trainer immediately repeats the verbal command. This procedure is repeated until all of the basic tasks are under verbal stimulus control.

Criterion is standard on any five of the six body parts. Care must be taken to randomize the presentation of items in all training sessions. In the Teach-steps, mastered items are interspersed with the new one.

The non-criterion tasks associated with this part are the commands:

Stand up.

Sit down.

Fold your hands.

Comb your hair.

Brush your teeth.

Wipe your nose.

Close your eyes.

Wash your ears.

These tasks are taught first as behaviors to imitate and then as actions to perform in response to verbal commands. They are to be performed in a "pretend" fashion; however, the trainer may wish to use a set of props including a comb, toothbrush, tissue, and a washcloth. Although the props require frequent cleaning and replacement, their use is highly recommended. It is not necessary for all of the actions to be under imitative control before an attempt is made to get some of them under verbal control. The trainer should feel free to substitute other actions.

However, it is **not** recommended that an action be paired with more than one body part; i.e., do **not** include both *Wash your hands* and *Wash your ears.*

2.12   Pointing to Objects Named

In this part the child is required to point to the objects named by the trainer. For example, *Show me the ball, Show me the keys.* The objects included are: baby doll, ball, bell, car, comb, hat, keys, shoe. A criterion performance requires the child to point to the correct item in the presence of any two others. In the Teach-steps, however, the trainer is allowed to work up to this. Be sure that there are never more than three items on the table at one time. Criterion is standard using the eight objects.

The non-criterion tasks are:

Rock the baby.

Throw the ball.

Ring the bell.

Push the car.

Put on the hat.

Shine the shoe.

Props would include only a shoeshine cloth, in addition to the basic objects themselves. Use the same procedure as that described for the non-criterion tasks in 2.11. **The next part must not be entered until the child has mastered this one.**

2.12a   Finding Concealed Objects Named: One Box

The child will have learned to point to objects named when three objects are placed in front of him in 2.12. Here all eight objects are spread on a table but are concealed under a cloth. The trainer shows the child the objects and then covers them. The child is then told *Find the_____*. The child is required to lift the cloth and to point to the item named. Items missed on the I-I are to be added one at a time in training sessions until all items are included. Criterion is standard.

The non-criterion tasks are the same as for 2.12.

2.13   Pointing to Room Parts Named

Here the child learns to point to the room parts named by the trainer. For example, *Show me the chair.* The room parts included are: box (a hatbox with lid), chair (use an **extra** chair), door, floor, light (the ceiling fixture), and the table. "Window" is **not** used because the children tend to become distracted when they look at a window.

The non-criterion tasks are:

Put the keys on the chair.

Close the door.

Mop the floor.

Turn off the light.

Wash the table.

Put the comb in the box.

Props might include a mop and a damp rag.

Options upon completion. If all parts of this phase are completed, or if the 10-Session Rule requires that you go beyond the phase, two options are available: (1) Vocal Imitation and/or (2) Receptive Expansion. Ideally, all options should be exercised as they become available to the child. But, if time does not permit, the trainer must make the choice on the basis of his prediction of the most immediate success for the child; i.e., performance on the I-I's.

2.20   RECEPTIVE EXPANSION PHASE I

The purpose of this phase is to teach appropriate responses to a variety of commands which make use of the vocabulary items introduced in 2.10. In addition, the child learns to respond appropriately to *Show me the_____, Find the_____,* and *Give me the_____.*

The trainer should administer the I-I's for 2.21, 2.22, and 2.23 before initiating any training in this phase. All three options are available. However, if training time is limited, the part on which performance is best should be entered first. If entry into any of the three parts is delayed, Retention Checks on the related parts in the Basic Receptive Phase should be administered and re-training initiated if necessary prior to introducing the parts in this phase. **Part 2.22a may not be entered until the criterion tasks in 2.22 have been mastered.**

The non-criterion task for this phase is a match-to-sample task which involves (1) matching objects to objects, (2) matching objects to pictures, and (3) matching pictures to pictures. Performance on this task does not affect criterion performance on any part in the phase. It is included to facilitate retention and also to begin to establish matching to sample—a basic teaching procedure. Further, if the child can recognize pictures, as opposed to objects, much time may be saved in subsequent Retention Checks by using pictures rather than real objects. Pictures are used only for retention purposes. **New tasks are always taught with real objects.**

2.21   Performance of Action Named: Body Parts

In this part the child learns to respond differentially to the following commands involving body parts:

> *Wash your ears.*
>
> *Wash your hands.*
>
> *Wash your face.*
>
> *Brush your teeth.*
>
> *Brush your hair.*
>
> *Comb your hair.*
>
> *Wipe your nose.* (tissue)

Wipe your mouth. (paper napkin)

Close your eyes.

Open your eyes.

Fold your hands.

Stand up.

Sit down.

The I-I includes two presentations of all commands in a random order with the exception of *Open your eyes* which must follow *Close your eyes.* Again, props may or may not be used depending on the situation. Criterion is met when 10 of the 13 commands are consistently performed correctly. At least the same 10 out of 13 tasks must be correct on 2 successive days or sessions.

"Face" and "mouth" are taught first as vocabulary items as in 2.11. "Face" is easily taught by making a circular gesture with the hand moving around the face without touching it. "Mouth" can be taught most easily with mouth open and with one finger pointing into the oral cavity.

The match-to-sample non-criterion task progresses in three steps:

1. A baby, a car, and a shoe are used for object-to-object, match-to-sample tasks. The trainer lays the three objects on the table. Then he shows the child a duplicate of one of the objects and says *This is a shoe. Show me another shoe.*

2. The same three objects are pictorially represented on large plastic-covered or coated sheets with black backgrounds. Best results will be obtained with large, colored, realistic representations of the objects. The trainer lays the three pictures flat, face up on the table and says *Look; this is a comb*, while picking up the comb and placing it on the picture of the comb. Then he picks up the comb, hands it to the child, and says *You do it.* Ultimately the child should be able to place any object on the correct picture with three

pictures to choose from in response to *Look. This is a* _____ . *Show me another* _____. Be careful to rearrange the pictures in random order and to present the objects to the child in random order.

3. Substitute pictures for the objects one at a time until the child can match picture to picture for all three items in any order or arrangement.

2.22 Performance of Action Named: Objects

Here the child learns to respond differentially to the following commands involving the objects:

> *Push the car.*
>
> *Rock the baby.*
>
> *Throw the ball.*
>
> *Ring the bell.*
>
> *Shine the shoe.*
>
> *Put on the hat.*
>
> *Take off the hat.*
>
> *Put on the shoe.*
>
> *Take off the shoe.*

It is important that the "put on" and "take off" tasks be interspersed with others; for example, the child may keep the "hat on" while he "rings the bell" and "rocks the baby."

It helps to use a shoe large enough for the child to put on over his regular shoe; lacing and tying are not required. Criterion is standard on 7 out of the 9 commands.

The non-criterion task for this part is simply a continuation of that for 2.21. Again, the key phrase is *Look; this is a* _____. *Show me another* _____. Start with three items: baby, car, and shoe; extend to other objects as the 10-Session Rule permits.

2.22a Finding Concealed Objects Named: Two Boxes

In this part the child learns to search for the object named in one or the other of the two boxes. Use the same objects as in 2.22. Two boxes are placed on the table side by side. The child watches as the trainer places one object in a box. The trainer replaces the lid and says *Find the_____*. The box used should be randomized. When the child finds the object, the trainer takes it out of the box and starts over with another object. No attempt should be made to confuse the child by moving the boxes about or by putting more than one object in the box at a time. Criterion is standard.

The non-criterion task associated with this part is the same as the basic task except that *Show me the_____* and *Give me the_____* are interspersed with *Find the_____*. The trainer should randomize his use of the different phrases. No distinction between *Find the_____* and *Show me the _____* is required. Note, however, that *Give me the _____* requires that the child **remove** the object from the box and give it to the trainer. The other carrier phrases simply require that the child remove the lid from the box and point to the object or display it in some appropriate manner to the trainer.

2.23 Performance of Action Named: Room Parts

The child learns to respond differentially to the following commands involving room parts:

Put the keys on the chair.

Put the baby on the chair.

Open the door.

Close the door.

Mop the floor.

Sweep the floor.

Turn off the light.

Turn on the light.

Wash the table.

Put the comb in the box.

The addition of a broom will be required. Criterion is standard on 8 of the 10 actions.

The non-criterion tasks associated with this part require the child to place the baby and the keys in prepositional relationship to the chair, table, floor, and box.

Put the keys on the chair.

Put the baby on the chair.

Put the keys on the floor.

Put the baby on the floor.

Put the keys on the table.

Put the baby on the table.

Put the keys in the box.

Put the baby in the box.

After performance is initially assessed, new commands should be added one at a time. After each correct response, the trainer removes the object **after** reinforcing the child. Commands should be randomized.

2.30   RECEPTIVE EXPANSION PHASE II

This phase introduces a variety of tasks involving simple receptive expansions that are assumed to be within the grasp of the children at this point and assumed to be likely to set the stage for the occurrence of two-word responses in the future.

The trainer should administer I-I's on all parts of the phase prior to initiating training. Although four options are initially available, the trainer should work first, if time is limited, on the parts where the I-I's show the greatest percentage of correct responses.

2.31   Discriminating Possession: Body Parts

Here the child is required to respond differentially to such commands as *Show me the baby's nose* and *Show me Tommy's nose,* using the child's own name with a possessive inflection. The child must point to the correct body part on the correct person.

This part is not as simple as it may seem. It may be necessary to review 2.11 Pointing to Body Parts Named and to first teach the commands using only the doll's body parts. Next, if need be, the trainer may teach the discrimination between the child's own name and baby; e.g., *Show me Tommy, Show me baby.* Finally, the trainer begins to randomize all body parts, mixing "the baby's" with "Tommy's." Use the basic body parts previously taught: ear, eye, face, hair, hand, mouth, nose, and teeth. Criterion performance is standard on each body part paired randomly with each "person." Both "persons" are more or less equally represented in the trial sequence. In this part, the understanding of person is more important than that of body part since most of the body parts already should be in the child's repertoire. If there is one body part, for example, ears, which is consistently confused with another, such as eyes, errors produced by this confusion should not prevent the child from meeting criterion. The trainer simply drops either ears or eyes, makes a note on the data sheets, and goes on.

If criterion is met in fewer than 10 sessions, teach knees, feet, arms, and legs as non-criterion tasks. In addition, try taping a large sheet of brown wrapping paper to the wall. Have the child stand against it, legs and arms slightly apart. Trace around him with a wide-tipped marking pen. Have the child stand back. Now go through all body parts previously taught. Say *Show me your _____.* Draw in the details as the child attempts to point them out on the outline of his body.

Remember that in each session in which you work on a non-criterion task, the child must at the beginning of the session give you a criterion performance on the basic task. In this way, both the purpose of retention of the basic task and anticipation of later content are served.

2.32 Placing Objects in Prepositional Relationship to Room Parts

This part is concerned with the spacial relationship between objects and room parts. The eight objects are paired in various ways with four room parts: box, chair, floor, and table. Three different prepositions are used: in, on, and under. The resulting commands are:

Put the _____ **in** *the box.*

Put the _____ **on** *the chair.*

Put the _____ **under** *the chair.*

Put the _____ **on** *the floor.*

Put the _____ **on** *the table.*

Put the _____ **under** *the table.*

The I-I is a random sequence of two trials on each of the six commands using a random sample of the eight objects. All objects need not be paired with each command. If the I-I does not provide at least two correct responses, intersperse training trials on prepositional relationships with trials on pointing to room parts. The child must eventually respond correctly to any triad of object, room part, and preposition.

One sequence of prompts which may be effective in minimizing errors in the Teach-steps is:

Show me the ball.

Show me the box.

Put the ball **in** *the box.* (Point into the box.)

Put the ball **in** *the box.* (Do not point into the box.)

The important aspect of this part is the prepositional relationship; therefore, the number of different objects used is not of crucial importance on criterion performance. Criterion is standard on the six commands using a random sample of the eight basic objects.

If criterion is met in fewer than 10 sessions, as a non-criterion task do a Retention Check on 2.13 Pointing to Room Parts Named and teach wall, line, and circle as vocabulary items. Look at 2.41 for directions on line and circle. Administer a Retention Check on 2.23 Performance of Action Named: Room Parts, and add:

> *Knock on the door.*
>
> *Touch the wall.*
>
> *Walk on the line.*
>
> *Walk around the circle.*

2.33 Giving Related Object Pairs

This part involves teaching a limited vocabulary expansion of the object category to include socks, coat, and brush, and teaching the child to give the trainer two related objects on command: *Give me the_____and the _____.* The related pairs used are:

comb—brush	brush—comb
shoe—sock	sock—shoe
hat—coat	coat—hat

The I-I includes (1) the six items taken **one at a time,** two trials each, and (2) the related object **pairs,** two trials each. If necessary, the new vocabulary items are taught singly using the same procedure as for 2.12. The trainer proceeds to train on the related object pairs only after the child has mastered the items taken one at a time.

Training trials on related object pairs consist of presenting each related pair of objects with **one** other object which may be any of the four other available objects; e.g., place hat, coat, and sock on the table in front of the child. The trainer then says *Give me the hat and the coat.* Care should be taken to reposition the objects on each trial. On any one trial the third object is randomly selected from the pool of four other objects. This task is a prerequisite to a memory expansion task involving unrelated objects. If standard criterion is met in fewer than 10 sessions, go right on to 2.33a Finding Concealed Object Pairs.

2.33a   Finding Concealed Object Pairs: Toy Box Search
This part involves the same related object pairs used in 2.33. All six objects are placed in a box and the lid replaced. Then the trainer says *Give me the _____and the _____,* asking only for related pairs. After the child removes the lid, gives the trainer the two objects and is reinforced, the trainer puts the objects back into the box, replaces the lid, and then asks for another related object pair.

Criterion is standard using each object pair in each order at least twice. If criterion is met in fewer than 10 sessions, intersperse requests for related object pairs with requests for unrelated object pairs using the same six objects as a non-criterion task. The trainer should take care to vary the order in which he asks for the objects within the pair; e.g., shoe-hat, hat-shoe. The unrelated object pair task is difficult. Therefore, be sure to intersperse trials on unrelated pairs with trials on related pairs.

2.34   Sorting Colors
On this task the trainer starts with only two colors to sort (use 1" color cubes) and builds up to 100% correct on a seven-color sort. The seven colors ultimately used may be selected from red, green, blue, yellow, black, white, purple, brown, and orange. The task involves presenting a container of mixed color cubes to the child. The child is told *Sort the colors,* into small containers. One entire sort constitutes one trial; therefore, in the early stages it is best not to give the child too many cubes at once. The child should not be interrupted during a sort unless he stops working. All corrections should be made at the end of a sort and after the child stops working. Many children will spontaneously correct sorting errors at the end. To the extent that self-correction is an ultimate goal, it is unwise to force correction earlier if it will occur spontaneously later.

When teaching the child to sort, the trainer gives the child a number of cubes of each of two colors and two small containers such as box lids. The trainer says *Put the red ones here* as he places a red cube in one of the small containers. The trainer then does the same with a cube of the other color, thus providing the child initially with a sample of each color to match. When the child masters the two-color sort, additional colors are added up to seven.

If the child at any point begins to make systematic errors in sorting colors, the trainer should eliminate the most recently introduced color that is being confused. Another color, not yet added, may then be substituted; or the trainer may back up to a two-color sort involving the color that is being confused and another color that offers the greatest contrast. The two-color sort can then again be gradually extended to the seven-color sort. Specific color confusions may be dealt with in a variety of ways. The important thing is to back up to success and only then try to move forward.

Note that this task does not readily fit the data sheet. Cross out Token Exchange Behavior. Describe the task and the quality of the child's performance. **Do not attempt to use the grid.**

Criterion is a 100% correct seven-color sort using at least five cubes of each color on two successive days. If criterion is met in fewer than 10 sessions, have the child sort objects, such as pencils, on the basis of color as a non-criterion task.

2.40   RECEPTIVE EXPANSION PHASE III

The parts of this phase expand the basic noun vocabulary and teach the child to follow more complex commands. In addition, an effort is made to set the stage for expressive responses that will enable the child to exert verbal control over the behavior of others.

2.41   Verb + Adverbial Place-Where Commands: Body/Space Awareness

In this part the child is taught to follow a variety of new

commands which require him to move his body through space. In the execution, the trainer must be up and moving about the room, a condition which complicates data collection and token dispensing. If no assistant is available, the trainer should be able, with a little practice, to reconstruct the events in the session from a tape recording. The trainer's verbal behavior should specify the responses to be made by the child; and the verbal reinforcement he gives the child should describe the child's responses. The activities involved in this part seem to be intrinsically reinforcing to most children; therefore, it is suggested that social reinforcers such as verbal praise, applause, smiles, and congratulatory "pats on the back" be used predominantly.

The activities require two large packing cases, one more or less square and the other preferably a refrigerator carton. A 10' length of rope and some black and white Mystic tape are also needed. Although it is not absolutely necessary, carpeting on the floor is desirable; a rug covering only part of the floor or even a blanket might serve as well. A few other easy-to-make items are described below.

The commands are:

Get in the box.

Look up. (Paste large cutouts of stars and moon on the ceiling.)

Look down. (Put colored tape across the toes of child's shoes.)

Fall down.

Stand up.

Turn round and round. (Do several 360° turns.)

Walk on the line. (Use Mystic tape to make 6' line on the floor.)

Walk around the circle. (Make circle out of rope on the floor.)

Get in the circle.

Crawl under the table.

43

Run to the wall.

Come to me.

Crawl through the tunnel. (Open both ends of refrigerator carton and position it on its side.)

In the I-I, F-I, Retention Checks, and Test-steps, the different commands should be presented in as random a manner as possible. After completion of each task, prompt the child to come to you in response to your saying *Come to me.* Praise him and then give him the next command. In the training steps, give the verbal command one time. If the child does not respond or responds incorrectly, give the command again and then perform the action; i.e., give the command plus an imitative model. If necessary, provide the child with physical assistance along with the verbal command. Later, the trainer can use gestural prompts as needed. Criterion is standard on at least one trial on each command in a random order.

Teach line, circle, wall, and tunnel as vocabulary items in the usual *Show me the_____* manner before beginning to train on the basic task. Training trials on these items should be interspersed with trials on the room parts already mastered. If the child meets criterion in fewer than 10 sessions, use the non-criterion tasks suggested for 2.32.

2.42   Vocabulary Expansion: Nouns

The vocabulary items in this part are taught exactly as in the Basic Receptive Phase. The items to be included are:

bread (real)

candy (real)

circle (drawn on paper)

cup

feet

fork

hammer

knees

knife

line (drawn on paper)

nail

napkin (paper)

paper (blank white sheet)

pencil

plate

soap (bar)

spoon

towel

tunnel (packing case open at both ends)

wall

water (in a drinking glass; child must touch the water)

Intersperse trials on new items with trials on previously mastered vocabulary items. Keep the density of reinforcement high. The child should be right on at least 50% of the trials in any one session.

The trainer must be extremely careful in administering this part. Add new items slowly. At the slightest sign of frustration or restlessness, the trainer should present a series of several trials on items that have already been mastered. If such care is not taken, the child may begin to make errors on previously learned items so that much time will be wasted on retraining. Be sure to note the occurrence of any appropriate extraneous responses, such as vocal approximations of the nouns. This information will be very useful in 3.51 Vocabulary Expansion: Naming Nouns.

It is not necessary for the child to master all items in this part at this time. Criterion varies as a function of the results of the I-I. In general, the rule is: Criterion is 21 minus I-I divided by 2, plus the I-I. For example, if the I-I is 5, the Criterion is 13 ($\frac{21-5}{2}$ + 5).

Number Correct on I-I	plus	$\frac{21-I-I}{2}$	equals	Criterion
0		11		11
5		8		13
10		6		16
15		3		18
16		3		19 (90%)
17		2		19
18		2		20
19		1		20

Pictures may be used; at first use only a few pictures and many real items. Gradually, it may be possible to replace all items with pictures. Remember that the use of pictures is a convenience to the trainer. The child is not required to respond to pictures. Therefore, errors made by the child as a consequence of using pictures are not to be considered errors. A criterion performance for the child is based on the use of real items.

There is no non-criterion task prescribed for this part. If the child meets standard criterion (19 correct) in fewer than 10 sessions, go right on to 2.42a Finding Object Named: Toy Box Search.

2.42a   Finding Object Named: Toy Box Search

All of the basic objects taught prior to 2.42 are placed together in a large box on the floor. The child is required to find the object named and to give it to the trainer who then places it on the table. If the child makes an error on the I-I, the trainer simply takes the item from the child and puts it back into the box. The items included are:

baby	comb
ball	hat

bell	keys
brush	shoe
car	socks
coat	

Criterion is standard. If the child meets criterion in fewer than 10 sessions, the trainer should gradually add items mastered in 2.42.

2.43   Sorting Big/Little

Here the child learns to sort objects by size. Provide the child with a quantity of big and little objects of the same kind. For example, use pegs made from 1" dowels and pegs made from ¼" dowels. A variety of things can be used but the objects must be the same except for size. The mixture should be placed in a shallow container. Give the child two containers for the sort. Follow essentially the same instructions as for color sorting. For example, first provide a model performance and say *Big* every time you place a big one in a container. Say *Little* when you place a little one in a container. Start the sort by placing one big and one little item in the two containers.

Criterion is 100% correct on a sort which involves at least 10 big items and 10 little items, on 2 successive training sessions.

The non-criterion task is the same as the criterion task except that different objects are used. For example, if dowels are used for the criterion task, big and little spoons might be used for the non-criterion task.

2.44   Pointing to Color Named

This task requires the child to point to the color that the trainer names. In the I-I, the trainer uses nine different 1" color cubes: red, green, blue, yellow, black, white, purple, brown, and orange. The trainer scatters the nine cubes on the table and then says *Give me*_____(color name). The cube named is not removed.

Criterion is 2/9 colors consistently correct in training sessions held on 2 successive days. Criterion is low because the primary reason for introducing colors is to set the stage, again, for a two-word response.

The basic task involving all nine colors is out of sequence. However, many children acquire receptive knowledge of one or two colors quite early. The task is included here in order to set the stage for two-word noun phrases such as *Red car*. The I-I includes the nine colors because there seems to be no basis for predicing for any one child which colors, if any, may already be known or which colors are easier to learn than others.

In the Teach-step, it may be necessary to use only one color cube at a time to teach the child to point to the color cube named; that cube can then be replaced with another. Later the child can be taught to respond differentially to the two cubes at the same time. Gradually build up to at least three cubes. Be careful to frequently intersperse teaching trials with trials on already mastered items (either colors or some other mastered task). The F-I is the same as the I-I, 2/9 on 2 successive training days.

If criterion is met in fewer than 10 sessions, continue to teach additional colors as a non-criterion task.

2.50   RECEPTIVE EXPANSION PHASE IV

2.51   Verb + Noun + Adverbial Place-Where Commands: Ball

This part builds on the language tasks introduced in 2.41 Verb + Adverbial Place-Where Commands: Body/Space Awareness. All of the tasks involve the use of balls. The commands are:

Throw the ball in the box.

Throw the ball up.

Roll the ball through the tunnel.

Throw the ball at the wall. (Mark a section of wall as a target.)

Throw the ball to me.

Put the ball in the circle.

In the I-I and F-I criterion is standard, or no more than 2 errors in the 14-trial sequence. In training, use gestural prompts, imitative models, and physical assistance as needed.

As in 2.41, this part does not lend itself to systematic token dispensing or data collection during the training steps. Follow the same procedures used in 2.41.

If criterion is met in fewer than 10 sessions, intersperse trials on 2.51 with trials on 2.41 as non-criterion tasks.

2.52   Verb + Noun Commands: New Nouns
The tasks in this part require a variety of materials which are self-explanatory. For each trial, provide the child only with the materials needed for that trial. The commands are:

Hammer and nail. (hammer and board with nail already partially driven)

Tear the paper.

Cut the bread. (table knife)

Pour some water. (pitcher and cup)

Make a circle. (Magic Marker and paper)

Make a line. (Magic Marker and paper)

Make a tower. (five blocks)

Ring the bell.

Push the car.

Rock the baby.

Criterion is standard. Circle and line production need not be perfect—approximations will do.

If the child meets criterion in fewer than 10 sessions, as a non-criterion task the trainer should teach him to "Set the table" using knife, fork, spoon, plate, napkin, and cup. This can be done by marking the shapes of the objects on a place mat made of a large sheet of construction paper. After this is mastered, use an unmarked place mat. If prompts are needed, place cutouts of shapes in the appropriate places; and allow the child to place the objects directly on top of the cutouts. Try to teach items in the table setting as receptive vocabulary items (*Show me the* _____) if not already accomplished in 2.42.

2.53   Pointing to Big One

In this part the child is required to make a simple size discrimination on verbal command. On each trial the trainer places two similar objects on the table and says *Show me the* **big** *one.* There should be a dramatic difference in the sizes of the similar objects. Be careful to vary the right-left position in which the two items are positioned on the table. The items are: doll, ball, car, comb, hat, shoe, sock, spoon, nail, box. Place the balls in a box lid so they will not roll off the table.

Caution: Do **not** place more than two objects on the table at a time. Do **not** fall into a positional pattern of arrangement for the big and the little objects.

The basic task in this part gives the trainer an opportunity to expose the child to the denial form of negation. If the child is attending well to the basic task and appears to be mastering the task readily, try this. After each correct response is made, the trainer gives the child a token, says *That's right; big one,* and simultaneously points to the big one. Then the trainer points to the little one, says *No big,* and simultaneously shakes his head. If this procedure seems to result in errors, discontinue.

Criterion is standard on the 10 object pairs. If the child meets criterion in fewer than 10 sessions, as a non-criterion task place **two object pairs** on the table at once and ask for the big _____. For example, arrange the big and little dolls and the big and little boxes on the table; the trainer then says *Show me the big baby,* or *Show me the big box.*

50

2.54 Give Me 1-5

This part involves only five commands: *Give me one. Give me two*, up to *Give me five.* Line up five tokens on the table in front of the child. The I-I is a randomized sequence of two trials on each command with criterion as standard.

For training purposes, cut out five poster-board cards, 3" x 8", and trace around the tokens: one circle on one, two on another, three on another, up to five. If a prompt is needed, present the appropriate card and repeat the verbal command. The child places the proper number of tokens on the card. If the child can count, he should at first count the tokens aloud as he performs this task. The trainer then teaches him to inhibit vocal counting except on the number requested. For example:

Trainer:	*Give me three.*	
Child:	*One, Two, Three.*	Child hands three tokens to the trainer.
Trainer:	*Good.*	Trainer whispers *One* and *Two* and then says *Three* quite loudly.
Child:		Child imitates.

If child meets criterion in fewer than 10 sessions, use multiples of various objects such as small plastic combs, pencils, keys, knives, forks, spoons. Several non-criterion tasks can be attempted:

1. Same as for basic task except use objects rather than tokens. (Do not use card prompts, however.)

2. Place two sets of five objects on the table and say *Give me two spoons; Give me four pencils*, etc. The child must select the correct number and the correct object.

3. Increase the number of duplicate items to 10 but otherwise use the same procedure as in the basic task; i.e., request only from one to five objects.

Once the child has mastered the basic task in this part, the trainer should place specific token values on the various items available at token exchange time.

2.55   **Pointing to Color + Object Named**

The child is confronted with similar objects of different color in this part. There is no need to represent every object in every color. Only colors mastered in 2.44 Pointing to Color Named should be used with at least five different objects. The objects used may vary, but experience suggests that these are conveniently obtained in color.

> block (This is a new vocabulary item introduced before the other items are used.)
>
> ball
>
> car
>
> comb
>
> shoe
>
> sock
>
> paper (4" x 4" squares of colored paper)
>
> cup
>
> pencil
>
> line (colored line on white paper)
>
> circle (colored circle on white paper)

Several steps are involved:

1. Retention Check on colors in 2.44.

2. Retention Check on objects selected for use.

3. Repeat 2.44 using three blocks in each trial. Say *Give me the blue* block, etc.

4. I-I: The following is an example of a trial. Place a red comb, a green comb, a red ball, and a blue ball in a

box lid on the table in front of the child. Say *Give me the red ball.* Replace the object after each trial. These four objects yield four trials. Be sure to randomize the combination of pairs, the position on the table, and the order of the requests. Use at least five different objects as well as the colors mastered in 2.44; criterion is standard on 24 trials.

5. Training trials: Use all items correct in I-I and intersperse other object pairs one at a time until mastered. Try to keep the density of reinforcement for correct responses during training at about 75% or higher.

6. F-I: Same as I-I.

Criterion on this part is standard on 24 trials which include requests for all colors used at least twice. If criterion is met in fewer than 10 sessions, try to teach additional colors not mastered in 2.44 as a non-criterion task.

2.60   RECEPTIVE EXPANSION PHASE V

2.61   Vocabulary Expansion: Nouns (continued)

Resume training on 2.42. Administer F-I on no more than one category in any one session. Criterion is standard on no more than 10 items from the same category; category membership of items must be respected. Ultimately the child must meet standard criterion in every category.

If criterion is met in fewer than 10 sessions, explore the child's ability to respond to categorical names. For example, place three pictures in front of him: a glass of water, a hammer, and a car. Say *Give me something to drink.* Use the following categorical names for the non-criterion task:

something to eat

something to play with

something to drink

something to wear

something to eat with

something to ride in

2.61a Finding Object Named: Toy Box Search (continued)

This part is a continuation of 2.42a. In addition to the 11 objects used in 2.42a, include at least five additional items from 2.42. Criterion is standard on all 16 items.

If criterion is met in fewer than 10 sessions, use the same non-criterion task suggested for 2.61.

2.62 Pointing to Big/Little One

Use the same materials as in 2.53 Pointing to Big One. In the I-I, place one pair of objects on the table for each trial and say either *Give me the big one,* or *Give me the little one.* Remove both objects and present a different pair for the next trial. Criterion is standard on five trials on big and five trials on little.

In the training steps, the following procedure is effective:

1. Place one object pair on the table in front of the child and say *Give me the* **big** *one.* When the child returns the big one, place it in your lap, and then say *Give me the* **little** *one.* If the child fails to respond, repeat the command and nod toward the little one. Repeat this procedure with different object pairs until the child promptly hands over the little one. After each correct response, be sure to say *That's right. This is the* **little** *one.*

2. Place an object pair on the table in front of the child and say *Give me the* **big** *one.* When the child returns the big one, reinforce him and put the big one back on the table in the same place. Now say *Give me the* **little** *one.* If he fails to respond, repeat the command

and point to the little one. Continue until the child consistently gives you the little one on command.

3. Place an object pair on the table in front of the child and begin to randomize big/little commands. Correct responses are reinforced; errors are ignored. For example, if the child gives you the wrong item, replace the item, repeat the command, and point to the correct item. Reinforce the correct, prompted response.

3. Keep the density of reinforcement high—about 75% by interspersing trials from Step 1 above.

If the child meets criterion in fewer than 10 sessions, present two sets of big/little objects and ask for big/little + object.

2.63   Pointing to 1-5 + Object

On poster-board cards, about 3" x 8", paste or draw different quantities of the same objects, 1-5. Many of the vocabulary items are relatively easy to draw, for example: eyes, ears, hands, ball, bell, comb, hat, keys, box, chair, door, light, table. Prepare at least five different sets to start with and add to these as you can. This task can assist in maintaining the now rather large receptive noun vocabulary. In addition, the child learns to identify the rather crude and cryptic pictorial representation of the objects.

The I-I consists of placing two cards from any set of five and one card from another set of five in front of the child on the table. For example, the trainer says *Give me two keys* in the presence of the two-key card, the five-key card, and the two-box card. Criterion is standard on five different quantity card sets (there should be 25 cards, five different sets); all quantities, 1-5, should be presented at least twice in no more than 24 trials.

In the training trials, the trainer may wish to start by using only two cards at a time; for example, two-key card vs. five-key card. Then on the next trial use the two-key card vs.

the two-box card. Finally, use the three together, always asking for the two-key card. The trainer may prompt by saying *Show me the keys*; and the child should be allowed to count if he can.

The F-I is the same as the I-I. If the child masters the task in fewer than 10 sessions, add additional five-card sets.

Caution: This part does **not** require the child to recognize Arabic numerals or numbers in written word form. An example of one set of five cards is presented below:

3" | 0 | | 00 | | 000 | | 0000 | | 00000 |
8"

3.00

Verbal Section – Expressive

3.10   VOCAL IMITATION PHASE

The child may enter the Verbal Section—Expressive as soon as he meets criterion on the Basic Receptive Phase. He must enter via 3.10 Vocal Imitation. The purpose of this phase is to teach the child to differentially imitate at least 10 of the 20 basic vocabulary items used in the Basic Receptive Phase. The child need only approximate the correct articulation; perfection is not the goal. Remember that normal children begin to talk with less than perfect articulation. The trainer works to obtain consistently recognizable imitations of the words. Final criterion is met when the child consistently imitates at least 10 of the 20 words in a randomized test, 2 trials on each word, in such a way that the trainer can recognize the words.

The procedure for I-I, Test-Teach steps, F-I, and Retention Checks remains the same as for other parts described earlier. The trainer says *Do this; say* _____. If the I-I yields any correct responses, the trainer has a place to begin with words. On new imitative responses the trainer first attempts to get an approximation of whole words. Words for training are selected on the basis of their likelihood of success. First get the correct or near-correct production under good stimulus control. If possible, it is important that the child be able to produce one or two correct responses in order that these can be interspersed with training trials on words that are only approximated. When deciding upon new words for training, it is sometimes worthwhile to repeat the I-I in order to see whether words not previously produced correctly or approximated have come under better imitative control. Extraneous responses recorded during administration of the Basic Receptive Phase should also be considered.

Only if the child does not respond to whole-word stimulation should the trainer back up to establish vocal imitation on a less demanding level. There are five back-up steps.

1. Try to get an imitative response to a syllable, such as /bʌ/ as in butter or /mʌ/ as in mother. Sit directly in front of the child but across a narrow table. Hold a block out to the side of your face as you utter the syllable. After the utterance, place the block on the table and pick up another. Continue the same routine, building a tower with the blocks. Go slowly. Continue even if the child begins to imitate. Let the child knock down the tower on command; if he doesn't, do it for him or assist him. Pick up the blocks and start again. Wait for a few seconds before you stack the block, holding it out to the side of your face. If the child says the syllable, show approval and stack the block. Continue, allowing the child to experience this success without additional demands. After several sessions, try to get the child to imitate words. Continue to intersperse trials on syllables as long as needed to maintain the density of reinforcement.

2. If there is no response to syllable imitation, encourage the child to imitate vowel sounds or any sound such as "mmm." Use the same basic procedures but, in addition, place one of the child's hands lightly on the throat when saying the sound. If the sound is voiceless, place the child's hand in front of your mouth so that he can feel the air stream. Stack the block; then place the child's hand on his own throat

or in front of his own mouth and wait. If nothing happens, continue as before. If the child vocalizes, show approval and stack the block. Continue the same procedure; accept any kind of vocal exchange. If there is any success at all, stay with it; let the child experience success at this level for several sessions before trying to intersperse syllables or words with the detached sounds.

3. If there is no success with detached sound imitation, teach the child to imitate mouth positions without sound. For example, try the mouth positions associated with /a/ as in father, /i/ as in feet, /u/ as in boot. When teaching the child to imitate the mouth positions, exaggerate the position in order to provide him with a better model. To establish a mouth position, physical prompts and a mirror may be useful. Begin with one position. After one position is well established, add another and alternate with the first. Proceed similarly with the third. It is important to teach a variety of mouth positions. If there is success at this level, reinforce it and allow the child to experience this success for several sessions. Do not try to add sound too quickly. If you do, the child may stop responding entirely.

4. There is one last back-up step before resorting to a manual expressive mode. Attempt to chain together a series of motor imitative responses ending in a vocal response;* for example, clap hands, stomp feet, and say *Boo*! First teach "clap hands" and "stomp feet." Give lots of social reinforcement. Get this chain well established; then add *Boo*! The trainer says *Do this* prior to the presentation of the model. If the child

---

* Howard N. Sloane, Jr., Margaret K. Johnston, and Florence R. Harris, Remedial procedures for teaching verbal behavior to speech deficient or defective young children, in Sloane, Howard N. Jr., Macaulay, Barbara D., *Operant procedures in remedial speech and language training* (Boston: Houghton Mifflin Co., 1968), p. 80.

begins to imitate the model before the trainer finishes his execution, the trainer stops and says *Wait,* accompanied with a hand gesture. Then the trainer begins again. When finished, he may point to the child and simultaneously nod. This final prompt should be faded out as quickly as possible. If this procedure is effective, teach the child to imitate several sounds, syllables, or words in the same manner; for example, clap hands, stomp feet, and say, *Go*! After several vocalizations are under imitative control in this manner, begin to break the chain. Drop the first component in the chain by requiring the child to imitate only one action plus the vocal response; finally the remaining action is dropped. Just say, *Say /mi/* as in me.

5. If all else fails, as it sometimes does, switch to the manual expressive mode; i.e., teach the child to imitate some manual motor responses that are "signs" for words (see Chapter 6, Sign Language). If, subsequently, the child begins to imitate spoken words, switch to vocal imitation and to vocal-verbal expressive training; however, it might be wise to continue simultaneously training in the manual expressive mode.

If the child does give adequate imitations for at least half of the words, he may proceed to 3.21, 3.22, and 3.23.

Interfering Behaviors
There are at least two other problems that can thwart the trainer in teaching vocal imitation or any other vocal expressive skill: (1) stereotyped vocal response and (2) echolalia. The following strategies are offered in dealing with these forms of interfering behaviors.

Stereotyped vocal responding. This behavior is easily identified. The child utters only one invariant vocal response on all occasions. The sound(s), the inflectional pattern, and the accompanying facial expression are essentially identical for any particular child. Upon completion of the Basic Receptive Phase, the most straightforward procedure is to begin immediately with the procedure outlined above for establishing various mouth positions without sound. Then proceed to add sound. By then, it will be possible to establish some whole-word response.

This procedure moves **very** slowly. It may be necessary to reinforce the child initially for being totally silent. If the child utters the stereotyped sound, the trainer looks away from him for a few seconds, allowing no opportunity for reinforcement. It is critical that at least three mouth positions be taught prior to the introduction of sound. The trainer is trying to set the stage for variability. Teach one sound at a time while interspersing trials without sound. At least three different sounds should be under good imitative control before any attempt is made to obtain whole-word imitation. This cannot be rushed. In the meantime, train in any receptive phase for which the child has the prerequisite skills; and train in the manual expressive mode as described in Chapter 6.

The manual expressive mode is desirable for such a child for two reasons: (1) it gives him an effective expressive mode, and (2) it seems to facilitate the acquisition of the vocal expressive mode. The trainer must be extremely firm in ignoring all stereotyped responses. And the trainer must be patient, moving in very small steps. In the meantime the child **may** advance rapidly in the receptive phases and in the manual expressive mode.

Echolalia. The procedure suggested for the elimination of echolalia has been described by Ausman and Gaddy.* In the receptive phases, echolalic responses can be ignored. The program is administered the same as for any other child. In the expressive training, the trainer states the question very softly and then states the desired verbal response very loudly. He then

---

* James O. Ausman, and Michael R. Gaddy, Reinforcement training for echolalia: Developing a repertoire of appropriate verbal responses in an echolalic girl, *Mental Retardation*, 1974, Volume 12, 20-21.

repeats the question softly and omits the answer. For example, in 3.22 Naming Objects, the trainer whispers *What is this?* and then says loudly *Car.* The trainer then repeats the question softly and waits for the child to answer. When the child repeats only the desired verbal response, he is reinforced with praise and edibles. As soon as possible, the trainer says only the question, requiring the child to supply the correct verbal response. This procedure can be used in all expressive phases; however, the trainer should not move past Expressive Expansion I, unless echolalia no longer occurs in the Basic Expressive Phase or in the Expressive Expansion Phase I. This will allow the trainer to use the 10-Session Rule moving back and forth between 3.20 and 3.30.

Throughout the expressive phases the trainer must remember that perfect articulation is not required. Any approximation to the correct response that the child utters is reinforced provided the trainer is able to discriminate among the different responses being made. If the trainer is unable to discriminate between two utterances, one of the items is dropped until a better approximation of the other can be established. For example, if the child's production of "ear" and "teeth" is a more or less identical "ee"/i/, drop "teeth" until "ear" is more clearly "ear."

The ability of the trainer to guide the child to closer and closer approximations of correct articulation as he moves through the expressive phases and their parts is likely to be highly variable. Professional consultation in this area is desirable and should be sought if available. If it is not available, however, the trainer should simply be patient, speak clearly himself, and praise the child's efforts. Much improvement is likely to occur as a function of repetitious stimulation in the basic vocabulary.

The trainer should not press the child for better approximations in an aggressive manner. Many children interpret the effort made to get them to say the same word over and over as punishing or as an indication of failure; emotional reactions are likely to result. Such episodes weaken the effectiveness of training and must be avoided. Punishment for failure suppresses trying. If, inadvertently, the child becomes upset in any part of expressive training, the trainer should back up to the content of a previously mastered **receptive** part, conduct a token exchange, and terminate the session for the day on a happy and successful note. Such episodes can be avoided to a large extent by interspersing trials on already mastered content.

Successful expressive responses will be enhanced if the child **looks** at the trainer as instructions are given. No untoward emotional reaction from the child is likely to occur if the trainer requests one or two repetitions of the response. If the trainer wants a better **response** from the child, however, the child is entitled to a better **model** from the trainer. So, the trainer should exaggerate his production of the word in order to make it as visible as possible. He should provide tactile cues whenever possible. If he resorts to training on detached sounds or syllables, such trials should be alternated with trials on whole words which the child can produce correctly regardless of whether the words are in the program (for example, hi, bye-bye, mama).

3.20   BASIC EXPRESSIVE PHASE

The child may enter the Basic Expressive Phase as soon as he meets criterion on Vocal Imitation. This phase teaches the names of body parts, objects, and room parts used in the Basic Receptive Phase. In each of the parts the child is required to respond appropriately to the trainer's question *What is this?* as the trainer displays or points to the object, body part, or room part. In the concealed object part the child watches the trainer place an object in a box and replace the lid and then responds appropriately to the question *What is in the box?*

The I-I in each part of this phase includes all of the behaviors in the part. Although the naming responses that are already in the child's repertoire need not be taught, they are included in all Test-steps and in the F-I's. The naming responses are taught in the training sessions using the Test-Teach procedure. When selecting the first (or next) item to be taught, the trainer should consider (1) any approximations to words uttered during the administration of the I-I, (2) any approximations to words uttered extraneously during training in the Basic

Receptive Phase, and (3) words imitated correctly in the Vocal Imitation Phase. After all naming responses of a part have been taught, a F-I is administered.

By the time the child enters the Basic Expressive Phase he should be on a token system. He should have the opportunity to exchange his tokens at the end of each session for a variety of items of his own choosing which might include ice cream, some form of candy, some form of salty edible such as potato chips or Cheezos, magazines, combs, hair ribbons, hair barrettes, small dolls, small cars, etc. **This is a part of the program.** There seems to be no more effective way to teach the child to mand or to specify his wants. Regardless of what the child chooses, he is also given (free of charge) a cup of juice or Kool-Aid.

In the execution of a token exchange the trainer is expected to occasion the following responses and to use vocal imitation in teaching them:

Trainer: *Who has tokens?*

Child: *I do.*

Trainer: *What do you want?*

Child: *Cheezo.*

Trainer: *OK. Give me your tokens.*

Child: Gives trainer his tokens.

Trainer: *Thank you.* Gives child Cheezos.

Child: *Thank you.*

Trainer: *You're welcome. Have some juice, too.* Trainer gives child cup of juice. Child consumes the juice and edible.

Trainer: *Where are your Cheezos?*

Child: *All gone.*

Trainer: *Where is your juice?*

Child: *All gone.*

Trainer:	*Do you want more? Say, More.*
Child:	*More.*
Trainer:	Trainer gives child more provided the child says *More*.

If the child chooses a non-edible:

| Trainer: | *Whose magazine is this?* |
| Child: | Child points to himself and says his own name or *Mine* whichever is more easily shaped. |

Be sure to note whether or not the child rejects certain choices. Set the stage for him to reject, if possible, a non-desired item and teach him to reject by saying *No*. For example, if the trainer has observed that the child usually chooses candy, offer him Cheezos:

Trainer:	*Do you want Cheezos?*
Child:	Child may not respond at all.
Trainer:	*Say, No.*
Child:	*No.*

If at any time the child gestures rejection of training materials, be sure to use this as an opportunity to teach *No*. *All gone* and *No*, as described above, are early forms of negation; and the token exchange situation affords the trainer an excellent situation in which to teach them. Progress toward the acquisition of these behaviors should be noted on the data sheet in the space provided for Token Exchange Behavior.

3.21 Naming Body Parts

The child learns to name the body parts used in 2.11 Pointing to Body Parts Named. The I-I, the F-I, and the Final Criterion follow the usual format. The trainer, in many instances, will need to use vocal imitation as a prompting device. He can initially back up the question *What is this?* with the command *Say, Nose.* The imitative prompt is gradually faded out. The trainer reinforces successive approximations to the desired response; intelligibility, rather than perfect articulation, is the goal. The trainer must be able, however, to discriminate among the child's productions. Typically, articulation improves gradually as the child progresses through the program. Criterion is standard.

3.22 Naming Objects

Though administered in the same manner as 3.21, the objects used here are from 2.12 rather than the body parts from 3.21. Again, vocal imitation can be used as a prompt if the child fails initially to name the object in response to *What is this?* and as a shaping device if the child's utterance is less than correct. Criterion is standard.

3.22a Naming Concealed Objects

Though similar to 3.22 in which the child must name the object, here he does not see the object. In the I-I the trainer shows an object to the child, places it in a box, covers the box and asks *What is in the box?* The trainer does this with each of the eight objects in a random order.

The following training procedures and prompts may be useful. The trainer presents an object to the child asking *What is this?* (this response has been taught in 3.22). The child responds correctly and is reinforced. The trainer then places the object in the box and shows it to the child asking again *What is this?* as he points to the object in the box. Again the child responds correctly and is reinforced. The trainer then puts the lid on the box and asks *What is in the box?* using prompts until the child responds correctly. The trainer uses these procedures until the child's response is correct with any object in the box when the lid is in place. Criterion is standard.

3.23 Naming Room Parts

This part is administered in the same manner as 3.22 except that the six room parts introduced in 2.13, rather than the objects, are named. Criterion is standard.

The non-criterion tasks for the Basic Expressive Phase include:

1. **Sorting Colors.** Test on red, green, blue, yellow, black, white, purple, brown, and orange. Use 1" color cubes. This procedure is described more fully in 2.34 Sorting Colors. See also 2.44 Pointing to Color Named and 3.41 Naming Colors.

2. **Counting to Five.** Use tokens to count. Arrange them in a row. Have the child point to and touch each token as he counts. Use vocal imitation chaining, fading to the command *Count;* for example:

   Trainer: *Do this; say, One.* Point to and touch the first token in the row of five.

   Trainer: *Do this; say, One, two.* Point serially to the first and second tokens, up to five.

When Counting to Five, do not allow the child to imitate until finished presenting the imitative model. If for any reason this non-criterion task is inappropriate for a particular child, any non-criterion task previously suggested may be used.

3.30 EXPRESSIVE EXPANSION PHASE I

The purpose of this phase is to teach the child to respond to question forms more complex than the simple *What is this?* used in the Basic Receptive Phase. The child now must respond to questions such as *Whose nose is this? What is on the floor? What is gone?* and *Where is the shoe?* In addition, the child is taught to mand the actions of the trainer. In all cases, the questions set the stage for two-word responses in later phases.

3.31　Discriminating Possession: Whose? with Body Parts

One or the other of two verbal responses is required from the child: *Baby* (or *Baby's*) or *Mine* (or child's own name). *Baby* has already been taught. When the trainer points to one of the doll's body parts and says *Whose _____ is this?*, the child is taught to respond *Baby's*. When the trainer points to one of the child's body parts and says *Whose _____ is this?*, the child is taught to say *Mine* or his own name. This latter response may not be in the child's repertoire and may have to be taught via imitation and/or prompts, such as pointing to the child.

The following prompting procedure is suggested. The trainer points to the child's nose and asks *Whose nose is this?* The trainer then provides an imitative model; *Say, Mine.* If the child intelligibly approximates *Mine*, the trainer gradually eliminates the use of the imitative model.

When the child gives the correct response *Mine*, the trainer should **not** respond *That's right, it's* **mine** or *That's right, it's* **yours.** Rather, the trainer should use the child's name: *That's right. It's Tommy's nose.* This latter procedure is used in order to avoid confusion and to emphasize the pairing of *Mine* with the child's own name. Once the child responds *Mine* to *Whose _____ is this?*, the trainer points to the **doll's** respective body part and says, *Whose _____ is this?* The trainer may either use imitation such as *Say, Baby's* or he may use the question form *What is this?* when pointing to the doll's body parts.

Though two-word responses are not required, the child has been taught the component responses needed to say *Baby's nose, My eye, Eye mine,* etc. For this reason it is particularly important to observe extraneous responses occurring during the administration of this part and to note whether such noun phrases do occur. The trainer should not be concerned about word order.

All body parts previously introduced in criterion tasks are used. Criterion is standard on each body part paired with the doll and child.

If the child meets criterion in fewer than 10 sessions, teach knees, feet, arms, and legs as vocabulary items; and attempt to teach the two-word responses *Baby's nose*, etc., and *My nose*, etc., as non-criterion tasks.

3.32 Naming Object in Prepositional Relationship to Room Part

Here the child is taught to name the objects (baby, ball, bell, car, comb, hat, keys, shoe) when the trainer positions the object and asks the questions *What is in the box?* (box uncovered), *What is on the chair? What is on the floor?* and *What is on the table?* The easiest prompting device is simply to point to the object and ask *What is this?* and then return to *What is in the box?* All objects should be taught with each of the four room parts. Criterion is standard for 20 trials including the 4 room parts at least 4 times.

If the child meets criterion in fewer than 10 sessions, as a non-criterion task attempt to teach the two-word responses resulting from object plus room part; e.g., *Ball floor.* Typically the normal child will omit the preposition at first. Obviously if you can obtain a three-word response, this is good!

3.32a Naming Missing Object: What's Gone?

In this part the child is taught to name a missing object. The child is shown one of the eight objects in a box. The trainer turns his back and removes the object, then turns around, points to the empty spot, and asks *What is gone?* The child is required to name the missing object. If necessary, let the child watch as you remove the object at first.

If the child meets criterion in fewer than 10 sessions, try to teach the two-word response resulting from object plus gone; e.g., *Shoe gone* as a non-criterion task.

3.33 Naming Room Part in Prepositional Relationship to Object

In this part the child is taught to name the room parts (box, chair, floor, and table) in response to *Where is the _____?*

including each of the eight objects. For example, the trainer places the hat on the floor and asks *Where is the hat?* The child is taught to say *Floor.* If the child has difficulty, the trainer may use an imitative model or point to the room part and say *What is this?* and then return to *Where is the _____?* The various objects should be positioned:

in the box

on the floor

on the chair

on the table

under the chair

under the table

Criterion is standard. All objects are not necessarily used. But any object used should be used in more than one prepositional relationship.

If the child meets criterion in fewer than 10 sessions, as a non-criterion task teach the two-word response involving object plus room part; e.g., *Hat floor.* As stated above, the normal child is likely to omit the preposition at first. Again, however, if the three-word response is obtained including the preposition, this is good.

3.34 Manding Actions: Verb-Noun

In this part the child is taught to say *Throw* and *Push* in order to get the trainer to throw the ball and push the car to him. First the trainer takes the ball some distance from the child and says, *Say, Throw.* After the child imitates the verbal response, the trainer throws the ball toward the child. Then he says to the child *Throw the ball.* If the child returns the ball, the sequence is repeated. The trainer holds the ball longer, waiting for the child to say *Throw* before giving him the imitative model. The child is gradually taught to mand the response of the trainer. In order to teach the child to say *Push,* the trainer sits on the floor, holding the car with the child sitting on the floor some distance from him. The trainer says, *Say, Push.* If the child says *Push,* the trainer pushes the car toward the child. If the child returns the car on command, the sequence is repeated. The same pattern as for the ball is repeated until the child mands the trainer's action without an imitative model.

Criterion is having the child mand the trainer's action to the ball and the car on at least two successive trials on each of the two objects in a given training session without an imitative model.

If the child meets criterion in fewer than 10 sessions in any 10-session sequence, the trainer should attempt to teach the two-word responses *Throw ball* and *Push car* as non-criterion tasks.

Success in getting other people to comply with our verbal requests is presumably a powerful reinforcer of verbal behavior. If the child can be taught to specify his wants, then he will have acquired a verbal skill that is likely to be reinforced in the natural environment. The task of teaching language then will be at least partially assumed by others; and the growth of the child's language will accelerate.

3.40 EXPRESSIVE EXPANSION PHASE II

The purpose of this phase is to teach the components of two types of noun phrases: color + noun and number + noun. In addition, the child is taught to utter two types of two-word noun phrases: (1) object + object and (2) object + (preposition + article +) room part.

3.41 Naming Colors

The trainer uses nine 1" solid color cubes: red, blue, green, yellow, black, white, orange, purple, and brown. In the I-I all colors are tested in the presence of all color cubes. The trainer points to a single cube on the table and asks *What color is this?* In the Teach-steps the trainer may teach one color in the presence of at first only that cube, gradually building up to the presence of the other eight. The trainer provides verbal prompts as needed. The F-I need not contain trials on all colors; however, all colors should be present on the table during the F-I. The trainer should first train on colors correct in the I-I, next on those that are most closely approximated in the I-I, and next on those that are most closely approximated in imitation.

Criterion is consistently naming correctly any 2 of the 9 colors in a random sequence of 20 trials (*What color is this?*), including each of the 2 colors at least 4 times.

There appears to be little basis for predicting which of the nine colors will be the easier ones to teach. However, any two colors can provide an adequate basis for training two-word noun phrases in the future.

If the child meets criterion in fewer than 10 sessions, teach the non-criterion tasks: (1) any colors not mastered and (2) two-word noun phrases involving the colors learned plus an object; e.g., *Red comb* in response to *What is this?*

3.41a   Naming Concealed Colors

The child watches as the trainer places one color cube in a box and replaces the lid. Then the trainer asks *What color is in the box?* The child is taught to name the color after it is no longer visible. To prompt, the trainer may simply remove the lid, allowing the child to look into the box, and repeat the question. Use only the colors previously mastered. Criterion is standard on 20 trials with each color being used approximately an equal number of times.

If the child masters the task in fewer than 10 sessions, as a non-criterion task the trainer should teach the child to name additional colors as in 3.41. Be sure to intersperse trials on colors being taught with trials on previously mastered colors.

3.42   Naming Two Objects

In this task the child is required to name two objects in series, in either order, in response to the question *What is in the box?* The child watches as the trainer places two objects in the box. The trainer tips the box toward the child and asks *What is in the box?* The child is expected to say the names of the two objects; e.g., *Ball, shoe.* The child is not expected to include the word "and." The trainer should say *and,* as it seems natural to do so. *That's right. Ball and shoe are in the box.*

Criterion is standard (appropriate two-word responses) on 20 trials involving random pairs of objects. In the I-I include the basic objects as well as those added in 2.33: baby, ball, bell, car, comb, hat, keys, shoe, sock, coat, brush. The F-I need not include all of the objects. Use only those that have been previously mastered. The trainer is testing whether the child names two objects in series; i.e., a **two-word response.**

If the child meets criterion in fewer than 10 sessions, as a non-criterion task try to teach him to include the word "and" (noun + and + noun). This is a difficult task and probably out of sequence; therefore, even a marker for the word "and" would be an impressive accomplishment. There is no need to include all objects or all possible pairings since the emphasis is on an effort to get "and" marked.

3.43 Naming Object + Room Part
in Prepositional Relationship

This part is the same as 3.33, except that the child is required to make a two-word response when the trainer asks *Where is the* _____ *(object)?* The child is only expected to say *Comb, table.* After the child's response, however, the trainer says *That's right. The comb is on the table.*

Criterion is standard on 24 trials which include at least 8 objects at least twice and every room part at least 4 times each.

If the child meets criterion in fewer than 10 sessions, as a non-criterion task try to teach him the three-word response object + preposition + room part. For example, the child should say *Comb* **on** *table,* in response to the question *Where is the comb?*

3.44 Counting to Five

Experience indicates that it is necessary for most children to learn to count objects before they can handle even simple number concepts receptively. The procedure for teaching counting is described earlier in 2.10 Basic Expressive Phase, non-criterion task. The same procedure is used here.

Criterion is 2 correct trials in the same session. The trainer lines up the objects to count tokens and says *Count.* The child is to simultaneously point to the tokens and say aloud *One, two, three, four, five.*

If criterion is met in fewer than 10 sessions, have the child count other like objects such as color cubes, pocket combs, pencils, etc., as a non-criterion task.

3.50 EXPRESSIVE EXPANSION PHASE III

3.51 Vocabulary Expansion: Naming Nouns

In this part, all of the basic expressive noun vocabulary is first reviewed. Retrain as necessary; then teach new vocabulary items as indicated below, including body parts, objects, and room parts taught in the Basic Expressive Phase. Identification of the items from pictures rather than objects is preferable at this point. The pictures should be photo-like, color representations. The use of pictures is suggested for two reasons: (1) pictures require an abstract type of response from the child, and (2) pictures are easier to manipulate than objects when a large number of items is involved. If the child can name **any** pictures of items, use the pictures and gradually replace the real objects.

Experience indicates that most children for whom this program is designed respond better to the real items than to the pictures of the items. Therefore, it is a good idea to intersperse trials using pictures with trials using real items. This procedure can be faded out as the strength of responses to pictures increases. Be sure to use real objects as back-ups. If the child fails to name the picture, give him the chance to name the real item before you give him an imitative prompt.

The expansion will result in the following categories and items. An asterisk indicates previously unlearned material.

Body Parts	Room Parts	Clothing	Toys
ears	box	hat	baby
eyes	chair	shoe	ball
hair	door	coat*	bell
hands	floor	socks*	car
nose	light		block*
teeth	table		
face*	wall*		
feet*	tunnel*		
knees*			
mouth*			

Edibles or Drinks*	Common Objects	Shapes*
bread*	comb	line*
candy*	keys	circle*
water*	brush*	
(plus items learned	towel*	
in token exchange)*	soap	
	nail	
	hammer	
	paper	
	pencil	
	cup	
	fork	
	knife	
	napkin	
	plate	
	spoon	

This list should be expanded further to include other nouns which have been emitted extraneously by the particular child. Certain items should be omitted if their production remains undifferentiated from the production of other items. Nevertheless, the expansion is likely to be extensive. At the first sign of emotional behavior, slow down. There is more to lose by pushing the child than by slowing down.

It is highly desirable to present the items within the framework of categories. The number of responses correct will tend to be higher if items are presented within categorical groupings than if they are presented in a completely random fashion. Furthermore, this procedure will set the stage for the child to learn categorical names and to sort the pictures into categories; these are abstract types of responses that are not readily acquired by severely retarded youngsters.

The I-I should respect categories, and no more than 10 items are inventoried at one time. Criterion is standard.

In the training steps, it is important to keep the reinforcement density high, at least 75% correct. Real items may be used to maintain this density.

Criteria on F-I should be established within various categories or sub-groups, enabling the trainer to move into 3.51a with at least some of the new vocabulary items. Enter 3.51a only with items mastered to standard criterion. F-I may be met on either pictures or real items, although pictures are more desirable.

If the child masters the content of this part in fewer than 10 sessions in any sequence, ask the question *What can you do with* _____? and assist him in supplying appropriate responses. This may be one of the prerequisites of categorization and a non-criterion task.

3.51a   Vocabulary Expansion:
What's Gone? with Three Objects

Only items mastered in 3.51 are used here, preferably within categories. The trainer places **three** objects from the same category into a shallow container of some sort, shows them to the child, turns his back, and removes one object, turns back around, shows the remaining objects to the child, and asks *What is gone?* The child is expected to name the missing object.

The I-I should consist of at least 10 trials using the vocabulary items established within a given category. The trainer should be careful to change the objects on each trial. Any category may be used. Criterion is standard.

In the Teach-steps, the following procedures may be useful:

1. Place one object in the tray. Show it to the child. Ask *What is this?* Reinforce, etc. Turn around and remove object. Turn back around and point to the empty space previously occupied by the object and ask *What is gone?* If no response, reach behind you and produce the object, asking *What is this?* When the child says the object name, again put it aside, point to the empty space and say *This is right. The_____ is gone.*

2. Once the child can name one missing object without promptings, place two objects in the box. Be sure that the two objects are from the same category. Prompt as in Step 1 above.

3. Add the third object and proceed as above.

The F-I and criterion are as described for the I-I. The non-criterion task is the same as that described above for 3.51.

3.52 Manding Action: Verb + Noun with New Nouns

This part is an expansion of 3.34 Manding Actions: Verb-Noun to include the content taught in 2.52 Verb + Noun Commands: New Nouns. Review and obtain a criterion performance on 3.34 first. Then inventory the actions listed below in the manner indicated.

> *Hammer the nail.*
>
> *Tear the paper.*
>
> *Make a tower.*
>
> *Ring the bell.*
>
> *Rock the baby.*

The trainer sits on the floor as in 3.34 and proceeds through *Push the car.* Now he picks up the bell. (Bell, paper, board-nail-hammer, five blocks, and the doll are on the floor behind the trainer.) The trainer says, *Say, Ring the bell.* If the child says either *Ring* or *Bell* (articles are unnecessary) the trainer rings the bell. The trainer goes through the other items similarly. As in 3.34, the trainer waits for the child to mand his response without an imitative model. Once the child gives a one-word mand, the trainer can gradually begin to demand a two-word mand.

Don't rush and spoil the fun. If it isn't fun, the child has no reason to participate. Note that *Throw the ball* and *Push the car* are included in the basic content of this part.

It is very difficult to arrange for severely retarded children to learn to mand. This is one of the reasons it is important to utilize the Token Exchange time for this purpose. It is also important to try to teach the child to verbalize any mands that are emitted through gestures.

Criterion is standard using the **seven mands.** If the child meets criterion in fewer than 10 sessions, as a non-criterion task teach him to say *What is this?* with respect to any assortment of objects. Point to an object and say, *Say, What is this?* If he responds correctly, name the object for him. Go to another object quickly. Whatever makes it fun and results in the desired response is the best procedure.

3.53   Naming Color + Object

Similar or same objects of different colors are needed for this part. Before starting, the trainer should review and obtain a criterion performance on 3.41 Naming Colors. In addition, the procedure used in 3.22 Naming Objects should be used with the objects selected to obtain a criterion performance on naming the objects.

The I-I here consists of placing two similar or same objects of different colors on the table in front of the child. The trainer points to one and asks *What is this?* The child must say "Color + Object." Include all color names mastered in 3.41. Use at least five different sets of objects. Criterion is standard.

In Teach-steps the trainer at first reinforces color **or** object naming, using vocal imitative models to evoke the two-word responses. Eventually only the two-word responses emitted without imitative models are reinforced.

The F-I is the same as the I-I. If the child meets criterion in fewer than 10 sessions, try this as a non-criterion task. Get out some plain white paper and two colored, felt-tipped marking pens. Children typically find marking with these pens highly reinforcing. Let the child observe you drawing with both pens. Then ask *Which color do you want?* Reinforce him appropriately if he names either color. If not, give him an imitative model. If he asks for a color, respond as he directs. Eventually, see what happens when he is given the non-preferred color. Does he reject it verbally?—through gesture?—or does he just take it? Remember to do this from time to time during Token Exchange. Assist the child in negating by using the word *No* as appropriate.

3.54   Counting Disappearing Objects 1-5

This part is a simple extension of 3.44 Counting to Five. The trainer should review and obtain a criterion performance on 3.44 before beginning this part.

For the I-I, the trainer takes out five tokens and lines them up on the table. He picks them up one at a time and drops them into a box with a slot cut in the top like a piggy bank. The trainer counts, as he drops them, *One, two, three, four, five.* Then he empties the box, gives the tokens and box to the child and says *Count the tokens into the box.* Provided the child has met criterion on 3.44, this task should present little difficulty. It simply assures the trainer that the child can count disappearing objects as well as objects that remain visible in front of him. Criterion is one correct performance of the task.

If the child meets criterion in fewer than 10 sessions, as he should, as a non-criterion task try to teach him to respond appropriately to *How many?* using 1-5 tokens or other objects. Suppress counting aloud on any but the last number in the appropriate sequence. Most children begin to count aloud in this situation; at first this should be reinforced. Provide him with a model, however, by whispering the number names that come before the last number. For example, set out three tokens and ask *How many?*

Trainer: *How many?*

Child: *One, two, three.*

Trainer: Whisper *One, two* and very loudly say *Three.*

Eventually, **point** only to one and two and say *Three* aloud. Do not expect the child to respond without counting. Sometimes they learn one, two, and three without counting but rarely is this the case for four and five.

four

Guides to Usage

To assist the trainer in using the program, two tables are compiled here to provide a ready summary of phases and parts. The first table, showing prerequisites and options upon completion, will aid the trainer in maintaining a proper program sequence. The second table, which is a brief description of each part, will aid trainers who already know the teaching techniques found in the text but wish to check criterion and non-criterion tasks.

SEQUENCING PHASES AND PARTS

Phase	Part	Prerequisite	Options Under Completion
1.10 Attending	1.11 Sitting Still	None	1.12 Interfering Behavior or 1.13 Looking at Objects, provided criterion is met on 1.12
	1.12 Interfering Behavior	Fails to meet criterion on 1.11	1.13 Looking at Objects
	1.13 Looking at Objects	1.11	1.14 Pre-Trial Eye Contact
	1.14 Pre-Trial Eye Contact	1.13	1.20 Motor Imitation
1.20 Motor Imitation	1.21 Specific Motor Imitation	1.14 Pre-Trial Eye Contact	2.10 Basic Receptive (2.11, 2.12, and/or 2.13)
2.10 Basic Receptive	2.11 Pointing to Body Parts	1.21 Specific Motor Imitation	2.12 and/or 2.13 if not already entered
	2.12 Pointing to Objects	1.21	2.11 and/or 2.13 if not already entered

82

Phase / Item	Prerequisite	Then enter
	2.12	and 2.12a
2.12a Concealed Objects		2.11 and/or 2.13 if not already entered
2.13 Pointing to Room Parts	1.21	2.11 and/or 2.12 if not already entered
		When all of Phase 2.10 is completed, then 2.21, 2.22, 2.23 and 3.10 Vocal Imitation
2.20 Receptive Expansion I	2.10 Basic Receptive	
2.21 Performance, Body Parts		2.22 and/or 2.23 if not already entered
2.22 Performance, Objects	2.10	2.21 and/or 2.23 if not already entered and 2.22a
2.22a Concealed Objects, Two Boxes	2.22	2.21 and/or 2.23 if not already entered

Continued on next page.

Phase	Part	Prerequisite	Options Upon Completion
2.20 Cont.	2.23 Performance, Room Parts	2.10	2.21 and/or 2.22 if not already entered
			When all of Phase 2.20 is completed, then 2.31, 2.32, 2.33 and 2.34
2.30 Receptive Expansion II	2.31 Possession, Body Parts	2.20 Receptive Expansion I	2.32, 2.33 and/or 2.34 if not already entered
	2.32 Objects to Room Parts	2.20	2.31, 2.33, and/or 2.34 if not already entered
	2.33 Related Object Pairs	2.20	2.31, 2.32, and/or 2.34 if not already entered and 2.33a
	2.33a Concealed Object Pairs	2.33	2.31, 2.32, and/or 2.34 if not already entered

2.34 Color Sort	2.20	2.31, 2.32, and/or 2.33 if not already entered
		When all of Phase 2.30 is completed, then 2.41, 2.42, 2.43, and/or 2.44
2.40 Receptive Expansion III		
2.41 Place-Where Commands	2.30 Receptive Expansion II	2.42, 2.43, and/or 2.44 if not already entered
2.42 Vocabulary Expansion: Nouns	2.30	2.41, 2.43, and/or 2.44 if not already entered and 2.42a
2.42a Toy Box Search	2.42	2.41, 2.43, and/or 2.44 if not already entered
2.43 Big/Little Sort	2.30	2.41, 2.42, and/or 2.44 if not already entered

Continued on next page.

Phase	Part	Prerequisite	Options Upon Completion
2.40 Cont.	2.44 Pointing to Color	2.30	2.41, 2.42, and/or 2.43 if not already entered
			When all of Phase 2.40 is completed, then any part in Phase 2.50

NOTE: If all parts except 2.44 are completed, options are any part in Phase 2.50, except 2.55.

Phase	Part	Prerequisite	Options Upon Completion
2.50 Receptive Expansion IV	2.51 V + Ball + Where	2.40 Receptive Expansion III	Any part in 2.50 not already entered
	2.52 V + New N	2.40	Same as above.
	2.53 Pointing to Big One	2.40	Same as above.
	2.54 Give 1-5	2.40 and 3.44	Same as above.

2.55 Pointing to Color + Object	2.40		Same as above.
			When all of Phase 2.50 is completed, then 2.61, 2.62 and/or 2.63

NOTE: If all parts except 2.54 and/or 2.55 are completed, options are 2.61 and 2.62.

2.60 Receptive Expansion V	2.61 Vocabulary Expansion continued	2.50 Receptive Expansion IV	2.62 and/or 2.63 if not already entered and 2.61a
	2.61a Toy Box continued	2.61	2.62 and/or 2.63 if not already entered
	2.62 Pointing to Big/Little	2.50	2.61 and/or 2.63 if not already entered
	2.63 1-5 + Object	2.50	2.61 and/or 2.62 if not already entered
			When all of Phase 2.60 is completed, continue with systematic Retention Checks on all phases and retrain as indicated.

Phase	Part	Prerequisite	Options Upon Completion
3.10 Vocal Imitation		2.10 Basic Receptive	3.20 Basic Expressive (3.21, 3.22, and/or 3.23)
3.20 Basic Expressive	3.21 Naming Body Parts	3.10 Vocal Imitation	3.22 and/or 3.23 if not already entered
	3.22 Naming Objects	3.10	3.21 and/or 3.23 if not already entered and 3.22a
	3.22a Naming Concealed Objects	3.22	3.21 and/or 3.23 if not already entered
	3.23 Naming Room Parts	3.10	3.21 and/or 3.22 if not already entered
			When all of Phase 3.20 is completed, then 3.31, 3.32, 3.33 and/or 3.34

3.50 Expressive Expansion III	3.51 Vocabulary Expansion	3.40 Expressive Expansion II	
	3.51a What's Gone?	3.51	3.52, 3.53, and/or 3.54 if not already entered and 3.51a
	3.52 Manding Action: New Nouns	3.40	3.52, 3.53, and/or 3.54 if not already entered
	3.53 Naming Color + Object	3.40	3.51, 3.53, and/or 3.54 if not already entered
	3.54 Counting Disappearing Objects 1-5	3.40	3.51, 3.52, and/or 3.54 if not already entered
			3.51, 3.52, and/or 3.53 if not already entered

When all of Phase 3.50 is completed, continue with Retention Checks on all phases and retrain as indicated.

NOTE: If the 10-session rule ultimately results in an impasse for color and/or number concepts, do not continue after all other parts are mastered.

This sequence is suggested to avoid the so-called "dead-end." If the sequence does not fit the child, change the sequence as it makes sense to you.

TASK DESCRIPTION

Part	Criterion	Criterion Task Description	Non-Criterion Task Description
2.11	Standard: 90% correct, 2 trials on any five items	**Pointing to Body Parts Named** ears eyes hair hands nose teeth *Show me Tommy's _____.* *Show me your _____.*	*Stand up.* *Sit down.* *Fold your hands.* *Comb your hair.* *Brush your teeth.* *Wipe your nose.* *Close your eyes.* *Wash your ears.*
2.12	Standard: 90% correct, 2 trials on each item	**Pointing to Objects Named** baby doll ball bell car comb hat keys shoe *Show me the _____.*	*Rock the baby.* *Throw the ball.* *Ring the bell.* *Push the car.* *Put on the hat.* *Shine the shoe.*

2.12a	Standard	**Finding Concealed Objects Named:** , Same as above.
		One Box
		Same objects as in 2.12
		Find the _____.

2.13	Standard	**Pointing to Room Parts Named**	*Put the keys on the chair.*
			Close the door.
		box	*Mop the floor.*
		chair	*Turn off the light.*
		door	*Wash the table.*
		floor	*Put the comb in the box.*
		light	
		table	
		Show me the _____.	

2.21	Same 10/13 items correct on 2 successive sessions, each item presented twice in each session	**Performance of Action Named:**	Match to sample:
		Body Parts	Object to object.
		Wash your ears.	Object to picture.
		Wash your hands.	Picture to picture.
		*Wash your face.**	
		Brush your teeth.	*Look. This is a _____.*
		Brush your hair.	*Show me another _____.*
		Comb your hair.	
		Wipe your nose.	Use same objects as in 2.12.
		*Wipe your mouth.**	
	Continued on next page.		

93

Part	Criterion	Criterion Task Description	Non-Criterion Task Description
2.21 Cont.		*Close your eyes.* *Open your eyes.* *Fold your hands.* *Stand up.* *Sit down.* *New Noun	Same as above.
2.22	Same 7/9 items correct on 2 successive sessions, each item presented twice in each session	**Performance of Action Named: Objects** *Push the car.* *Rock the baby.* *Throw the ball.* *Ring the bell.* *Shine the shoe.* *Put on the hat.* *Take off the hat.* *Put on the shoe.* *Take off the shoe.*	Same as above.
2.22a	Standard	**Finding Concealed Objects Named: Two Boxes** Same objects as in 2.12	Same task as in 2.22a criterion task. *Show me the _____.*

		Find the _____ .	*Give me the* _____ . *Find the* _____ .
2.23	Same 8/10 items correct in 2 successive sessions		**Performance of Action Named:** **Room Parts** *Put the keys on the chair.* *Put the baby on the chair.* *Open the door.* *Close the door.* *Mop the floor.* *Sweep the floor.* *Turn off the light.* *Turn on the light.* *Wash the table.* *Put the comb in the box.*	**Find the** _____ . *Put the keys on the chair.* *Put the baby on the chair.* *Put the keys on the floor.* *Put the baby on the floor.* *Put the keys on the table.* *Put the baby on the table.* *Put the keys in the box.* *Put the baby in the box.*
2.31	Standard		**Discriminating Possession:** **Body Parts** ears hands eyes mouth face nose hair teeth *Show me the baby's* _____ . *Show me Tommy's* _____ .	**Add:** knees feet arms legs Use wall-mounted body silhouettes. *Show me your* _____ .

Part	Criterion	Criterion Task Description	Non-Criterion Task Description
2.32	Standard	**Placing Objects in Prepositional Relationship to Room Parts** *Put the _____ in the box.* *Put the _____ on the chair.* *Put the _____ under the chair.* *Put the _____ on the floor.* *Put the _____ on the table.* *Put the _____ under the table.* Use the same objects as in 2.12	Retention Check on 2.13. Add: wall line circle Retention Check on 2.23. Add: *Knock on the door.* *Touch the wall.* *Walk on the line.* *Walk around the circle.*
2.33	Standard	**Giving Related Object Pairs** sock* shoe coat* hat brush* comb *Give me the _____ and the _____.* (Related pairs only.) *New nouns	Go right on to 2.33a.

2.33a	Standard	**Finding Concealed Object Pairs: Toy Box Search** Same objects as in 2.33; six objects in covered box. *Give me the _____ and the _____. (Related pairs only.)*	Alternate requests for related and unrelated pairs.
2.34	100% on 7-color sort on 2 successive days	**Sorting Colors** (using color cubes) red green blue yellow black white purple orange brown Sort the colors.	Sort like objects on basis of color.
2.41	Standard	**Verb + Adverbial Place-Where Commands: Body/Space Awareness**	Same as for 2.32.

Continued on next page.

Part	Criterion	Criterion Task Description	Non-Criterion Task Description
2.41 Cont.		*Get in the box.*	**Add:**
		Look up.	line
		Look down.	circle
		Fall down.	wall
		Stand up.	tunnel
		Turn round and round.	
		Walk on the line.	
		Walk around the circle.	
		Get in the circle.	
		Crawl under the table.	
		Run to the wall.	
		Come to me.	
		Crawl through the tunnel.	
2.42	See text	**Vocabulary Expansion: Nouns**	None.

bread	paper
candy	pencil
circle (on paper)	plate
cup	soap
feet	spoon
fork	towel
hammer	tunnel

knees wall
knife water
line (on paper)
nail
napkin

Show me the _____.

2.42a	Standard	**Finding Object Named: Toy Box Search**	Same as criterion task + appropriate items mastered in 2.42.
		baby comb ball hat bell keys brush shoe car sock coat	
		(All items in toy box)	
		Find the _____. (Child must hand object to trainer.)	
2.43	100% on 2 successive sessions	**Sorting Big/Little** Sort 10 big and 10 little objects; e.g., 10 big combs and 10 little combs, same color.	Same as criterion except with additional different objects.

99

Part	Criterion	Criterion Task Description	Non-Criterion Task Description
2.44	2/9 colors consistently correct on 2 successive sessions Only 2/9	**Pointing to Color Named** (using color cubes) red green blue yellow black white purple orange brown *Give me _____.*	Teach additional colors.
2.51	Standard	**Verb + Noun + Adverbial Place-Where Commands: Ball** *Throw the ball in the box.* *Throw the ball up.* *Throw the ball down.* *Roll the ball through the tunnel.* *Throw the ball at the wall.* *Throw the ball to me.* *Put the ball in the circle.*	Intersperse content of 2.41 with 2.51.

2.52	Standard	Verb + Noun Commands: New Nouns	Add:
		Hammer the nail. *Tear the paper.* *Cut the bread.* *Pour some water.* *Make a circle.* *Make a line.* *Make a tower.* *Ring the bell.* *Push the car.* *Rock the baby.*	knife fork spoon plate napkin cup *Set the table.* *Show me the _____ .*
2.53	90% of a series of at least 10 trials	Pointing to Big One Big and little object pairs, presented one pair at a time. doll comb ball hat shoe spoon sock nail car box *Show me the big one.*	Same objects as for criterion task, two pairs at a time. *Show me the big comb.* *Show me the big shoe.*

101

Part	Criterion	Criterion Task Description	Non-Criterion Task Description
2.54	Standard	**Give me 1-5**	Objects in multiples of five.
		Use five tokens.	*Give me two combs.*
			Give me five keys.
		Give me one.	
		Give me two.	etc.
		Give me three.	
		Give me four.	
		Give me five.	
2.55	Standard	**Pointing to Color + Object Named**	Teach additional colors not mastered in 2.44.
		(a) Retention Check on 2.34.	
		(b) Retention Check on objects selected for use.	
		(c) Repeat 2.44 saying, *Give me the blue block*, etc.	
		(d) Color + object; two objects + two colors in each trial.	

red
green
blue
yellow
black   Those mastered
white   in 2.34 and 2.44.
purple
orange
brown

       plus

block
pencil
line
circle   (at least five)
ball
car
comb
shoe
sock
paper
cup
Example: red ball, red sock, green
ball, green sock.
Give me the red sock.

Part	Criterion	Criterion Task Description	Non-Criterion Task Description
2.61	Standard	**Vocabulary Expansion: Nouns** Continuation of 2.42.	Categorizing pictures: *Give me _____ .* . . . *something to eat.* . . . *something to play with.* . . . *something to drink.* . . . *something to wear.* . . . *something to eat with.* . . . *something to ride in.*
2.61a	Standard	**Finding Object Named: Toy Box Search (continued)** Continuation of 2.42a; extend from 11 to 16 items.	Same as 2.61, non-criterion task.
2.62	Standard	**Pointing to Big/Little One** Big/little sets of five different objects; use one set at a time. *Give me the big one.* *Give me the little one.*	Same as criterion task except use two sets at a time. *Give me the big shoe.* *Give me the little comb.*

| 2.63 | Standard | Pointing to 1-5 + Object | Same as criterion task. |

Add:

Five sets of object cards, 1-5.

additional object card sets, 1-5.

Give me two keys, etc.

TOKEN EXCHANGE DIALOGUE

Who has tokens?	I do.
What do you want?	_____
OK. Give me your tokens.	(Gives tokens.)
Thank you.	
(Gives child _____.)	
You're welcome.	Thank you.
Have some juice, too.	
(Gives child juice.)	(Consumes juice.)

Where are your _____ ?	*All gone.*
Where is your juice?	*All gone.*
Do you want more?	*More.*
(Gives child more _____.)	
You're welcome.	*Thank you.*
Whose _____ is this?	*__(name)__ or Mine.*
Do you want _____ ?	*No.*
(non-preferred item)	

| 3.10 | 50% | Vocal Imitation | None |

Body Parts (6)
Objects (8)
Room Parts (6)

Do this; say _____ .

See text for back-up steps.

Part	Criterion	Criterion Task Description	Non-Criterion Task Description
3.21	Standard	**Naming Body Parts**	**Sorting Colors** (see 2.34)
			Pointing to Color Named (see 2.44)
		ear	Naming Colors (see 3.41)
		eye(s)	
		hair	
		hand(s)	
		nose	
		teeth	
		What is this?	
		or	
		What are these?	
3.22	Standard	**Naming Objects**	**Count:**
		baby	*One.*
		ball	*One, two.*
		bell	*One, two, three.*
		car	*One, two, three, four.*
		comb	*One, two, three, four, five.*
		hat	(Use tokens as objects to count.)
		keys	
		shoe	
		What Is this?	

3.22a	Standard	**Naming Concealed Objects**
		Same objects as 3.22 but concealed; one object at a time.
		What is in the box?
3.23	Standard	**Naming Room Parts**
		Same as 3.22.
		box
		chair
		door
		floor
		light
		table
		What is this?
3.31	Standard	**Discriminating Possession: Whose? with Body Parts**
		Same task.
		Add:
		ear
		eyes
		hair
		hands
		nose
		knee(s)
		feet
		arm(s)
		leg(s)
		teeth
	Continued on next page.	

107

Part	Criterion	Criterion Task Description	Non-Criterion Task Description
3.31 Cont.		*Whose* _____ *is this?* or *Whose* _____ *are these?* **Response** (one word): *Baby's* *Mine* *Tommy's* (child's own name)	**Response** (two words): *Baby's* _____ . *My* _____ . *Tommy's* _____ .
3.32	Standard	Naming Object in Prepositional Relationship to Room Part baby ball bell car comb hat keys shoe	Same task. **Response** (two or three words): Object + Room Part or Object + Preposition + Room Part.

		What's in the box? *What's on the chair?* *What's on the floor?* *What's on the table?* **Response** (one word): Child names object.	
3.32a	Standard	**Naming Missing Object: What's Gone?** Same objects as in 3.32; one object at a time. *What's gone?* **Response** (one word): Child names object.	Same task. **Response** (two or three words): Object + *gone* or Object + *is + gone.*
3.33	Standard	**Naming Room Part in Prepositional Relationship to Object** Same objects as in 3.32 *Where is the _____?* **Response** (one word): Child names room part (box, chair, floor, or table).	Same task. **Response** (two or three words): Object + Room Part *Baby chair.* or Object + Preposition + Room Part *Baby on chair.*

Continued on next page.

Part	Criterion	Criterion Task Description	Non-Criterion Task Description
3.33 Cont.		Place objects: in box on floor on chair under chair on table under table	
3.34	100% on 4 trials, 2 on each mand	**Manding Actions: Verb-Noun** **Response** (one word): *Throw* *Push*	Same task. **Response** (two words): *Throw ball.* *Push car.*
3.41	Any two of the nine colors (see text)	**Naming Colors** (using color cubes) red blue green yellow black orange purple	Same task; teach additional colors. *What is this?* **Response** (two words): Color + object *Red comb.*

brown
white

What color is this?

3.41a	Standard	**Naming Concealed Colors**	Teach additional colors as in 3.41.
		Colors mastered in 3.41; one color cube at a time.	
		What color's in the box?	
3.42	Standard	**Naming Two Objects**	Same task.
		baby	**Response** (three words):
		ball	
		bell	N + conjunction + N
		brush (Two objects at a time.)	*Ball and shoe.*
		car	
		coat	
		comb	
		hat	
		keys	
		shoe	
		socks	
		What's in the box?	

Continued on next page.

Part	Criterion	Criterion Task Description	Non-Criterion Task Description
3.42 Cont.		**Response (two words):** Child names objects. *Ball, shoe.*	**Response (three words):** N + preposition + N *Comb on table.*
3.43	Standard	**Naming Objects + Room Part in Prepositional Relationship** Same task as for 3.33. *Where is the _____.* **Response (two words):** Child names object and room part. *Comb, table.*	Same task.
3.44	Two correct trials in one session.	**Counting to Five** Use five tokens as objects to count. **Response:** Child serially counts five tokens. *One, two, three, four, five*	Count other like objects such as color cubes, pocket combs, pencils, etc.

3.51	Standard with variation; see text.	**Vocabulary Expansion: Naming Nouns** *What is this?* **Response** (one word): Child names noun (pictures).	Objects mastered in criterion task. *What do you do with _____ ?* **Response** (one or two words): *Comb hair.* or *Comb.*
		Body Parts ear new: face eye feet hair knee hand mouth nose teeth	
		Room Parts box new: wall chair tunnel door floor light table	
		Clothing hat new: coat shoe sock	

Continued on next page.

113

Part	Criterion	Criterion Task Description	Non-Criterion Task Description
3.51 Cont.		**Toys**	
		baby new: block	
		ball	
		bell	
		car	
		Edibles and Drinks	
		new: bread	
		candy	
		water	
		(plus items learned in token exchange)	
		Common Objects	
		comb new: brush	
		keys towel	
		soap	
		nail	
		hammer	
		paper	
		pencil	
		cup	
		fork	

		knife napkin plate spoon		
		Shapes		
		new: line circle		
3.51a	Standard in any one category			Same as above for 3.51.
		Vocabulary Expansion: **What's Gone? with Three Objects**		
		Items mastered in 3.51; three at a time.		
		What's gone?		
		Response (one word):		
		Child names missing item.		
3.52	Standard	**Manding Action: Verb + Noun** **with New Nouns**		**Response:** *What is this?*
		Throw ball. *Push car.* *Hammer nail.* *Tear paper.*		

Continued on next page.

115

Part	Criterion	Criterion Task Description	Non-Criterion Task Description
3.52 Cont.		*Make tower.* *Ring bell.* *Rock baby.* **Response** (two words) V + N: *Rock baby.*	
3.53	Standard	**Naming Color + Object** Minimum of five object pairs with colors mastered in 3.41 represented. Retention Check on 3.41 Retention Check on 3.22 *What is this?* **Response** (two words): Child names color + object. *Red comb.*	Two marking pens of different colors. *Which color do you want?* **Response** (one word): Child names color.

3.54	100%	Counting Disappearing Objects 1-5	*How many?* 1-5
			Use tokens or other objects.
		Retention Check on 3.44	
		Count the tokens into the box (bank).	
		Response:	
		Serial counting to five. Child counts token as he releases it.	

five

Inventory

by Erland W. Gleason*

The Inventory assists the clinician in determining a child's appropriate entry point into the program. It is not intended as a developmental measure of a child's language skills.

METHOD OF PRESENTATION

The trainer begins the Inventory at the first phase (Phase 1.00) and proceeds through all phases unless the child fails to meet the prerequisites required for the administration of a particular part of a phase. When administering the Inventory, the trainer carefully avoids the use of prompts, gestures or verbal cues since they may influence the child's performance.

The criterion for each phase and part is listed in the appropriate column on the right side of the Inventory. For example, if criterion is 9 correct out of 10 trials, it is represented as 9/10 in the Criterion column. The trainer records in the next column (Number Correct) the number of tasks correctly performed. For example, if the child correctly completes 7 of the 10 items, then 7 is put in the Number Correct column.

---

* Mr. Erland W. Gleason received his B.A. and M.A. from Michigan State University at East Lansing. He worked for two years in the public school system as a Speech Pathologist and has worked for three years with retarded children at Coldwater State Home, Coldwater, Michigan. He has presented papers to the Michigan Speech and Hearing Association and the American Association on Mental Deficiency.

Next the trainer indicates the child's success or failure on that particular part. A check (√) is placed in either the Pass or Fail Column.

The alphabetical letters in the Fail column indicate those parts of the Inventory which are to be omitted in the future if the child fails to meet criterion on a particular part. If the child fails a part which contains an alphabetical letter in the Fail column, the trainer omits testing on parts which have that alphabetical letter in the Prerequisite column. For example, if the child fails to meet criterion in part 2.12 Pointing to Objects Named, the trainer notes the letter B in the Fail column, returns to the Prerequisite column, and looks for parts which may be omitted. In the example, failure on 2.12 allows the trainer to omit testing on parts 2.12a, 2.22, 2.22a, 2.32, 2.33, 2.33a, 2.42a and 2.55. The child's ability to point to objects named is prerequisite to all of these parts.

SCORING
The trainer scores each item tested according to the following scoring key.

Correct	✓
Approximation	⊘
Incorrect	✕
No Response	○
Not Tested—Did not meet Prerequisite	NTP
Not Tested (for any other reason)	NT

Only **correct** responses are considered when determining whether the child has met criterion. A check mark is placed in the Pass column if he meets criterion and in the Fail column if he does not.

INTERPRETATION
Begin training in the phase preceding the first part on which the child fails to meet criterion. For example, if the first failure is on part 2.33 Related Object Pairs, training should begin in 2.20 Receptive Expansion Phase I. The strategy is

to back up to a firm level of success. A separate analysis of performance on the receptive and expressive phases must be made. The first failure point in both the receptive and expressive phases should be noted. A separate analysis allows the trainer to recommend entry points in both phases. When reviewing the results of the Inventory for a particular child, the trainer may note that performance on some parts is unexpectedly good or poor in relationship to performance on surrounding parts. This fluctuation may be a function of the child's past learning, or it may reflect an error in the sequencing. In any event, the trainer selects an entry point in the phase preceding the first failure (applicable for both the receptive and expressive phases). Once the child enters the program, no parts are skipped regardless of his performance on the Inventory. However, if the child clearly displays mastery of the entire program, the trainer should suggest another program.

PLOTTING THE RESULTS

The trainer plots the results according to the Sample Performance Graph illustrated in Figure 5 on page 123. The heavier line represents criterion performance. The second line is drawn by plotting the child's performance and connecting the points. The gap between the criterion line and the performance line indicates the areas needing improvement. The Inventory results, as displayed on the Performance Graph, aid the trainer in making the following judgments:

1. Assessing the LAP as a suitable training device for the child.

2. Determining where the training should begin.

3. Evaluating the degree of correspondence between the child's receptive and expressive performance.

4. Pinpointing islands of success or failure.

5. Detecting possible errors in sequencing.

6. Assessing improvement or retention from one testing time to another.

The Percentage Table below will aid the trainer when he first converts the child's number correct for each part into percentage scores. He simply notes the total number of items on each part of the Inventory and locates that number on the left side of the table. By reading across that line he locates the number of items correct for that part and finds the approximate percentage score directly above that number. If, for example, the child scores 9 items correct out of a total of 12, his percentage according to the table would be 70.

SCORING KEY

Correct Response	✓	No Response	O
Approximation	⊘	Not Tested	NT
Incorrect Response	X	Not Tested–Did Not Meet Prerequisite	NTP

PERCENTAGE TABLE

TOTAL NO. OF ITEMS	NUMBER OF ITEMS CORRECT AND PERCENTAGE CORRECT									
	100%	90%	80%	70%	60%	50%	40%	30%	20%	10%
6	6	5		4		3	2		1	
10	10	9	8	7	6	5	4	3	2	1
12	12	11	10	9	8-7	6	5	4	3-2	1
14	14	13-12	11	10	9-8	7	6	5-4	3-2	1
16	16	15-14	13	12-11	10	9-8	7-6	5	4-3	2-1
18	18	17-16	15-14	13	12-11	10-9	8-7	6-5	4	3-2
20	20	19-18	17-16	15-14	13-12	11-10	9-8	7-6	5-4	3-2
22	22	21-20	19-18	17-15	14-13	12-11	10-9	8-7	6-4	3-2
26	26	25-23	22-20	19-18	17-16	15-13	12-10	9-8	7-5	4-3
32	32	31-28	27-26	25-22	21-19	18-16	15-13	12-10	9-6	5-3
40	40	39-36	35-32	31-28	27-24	23-20	19-16	15-12	11-8	7-4
42	42	41-38	37-34	33-29	28-25	24-21	20-17	16-13	12-8	7-4
90	90	89-80	79-72	71-63	62-54	53-45	44-36	35-27	26-18	17-9

Figure 5   Sample Performance Graph

Child's Name _S. Kiener_   Birth Date _10·23·60_   Age _14·8_
Previous LAP Training (Mo.) _4 mos._   Last Training Phase _2.12_
Examiner _F. M._   Date of Evaluation _10·13·74_   Reliability _Good_

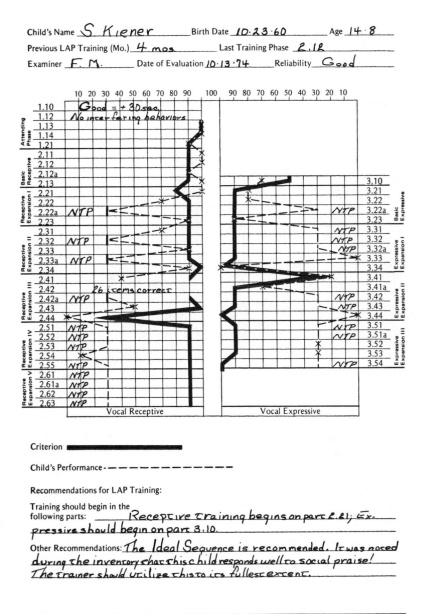

Criterion ▬▬▬▬▬▬▬▬▬▬

Child's Performance · — — — — — — — — — — —

Recommendations for LAP Training:

Training should begin in the
following parts: _Receptive Training begins on part 2.21; Expressive should begin on part 3.10._

Other Recommendations: _The Ideal Sequence is recommended. It was noted during the inventory that this child responds well to social praise! The trainer should utilize this to its fullest extent._

Figure 6   Performance Graph

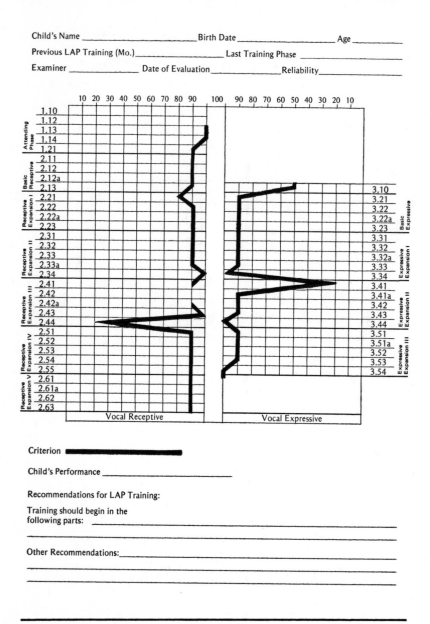

Child's Name _____ Birth Date _____ Age _____

Previous LAP Training (Mo.)_____ Last Training Phase _____

Examiner _____ Date of Evaluation _____ Reliability_____

Criterion ████████████████████

Child's Performance _____

Recommendations for LAP Training:

Training should begin in the
following parts: _____

_____

Other Recommendations:_____

_____

_____

	Criterion	Number Correct	Passed	Failed	Prerequisite
1.00 PRE-VERBAL					
1.10 Attending Phase					
1.11 Sitting Still	30 sec.				
1.12 Elimination of Interfering Behaviors ___ Body movement ___ Vocal behaviors ___ Hand movements ___ Self abusiveness	None				
1.13 Looking at Objects·(5 Random Objects)	10/10				
1.14 Pre-Trial Eye Contact (5 random objects)	5/5				

	Criterion	Number Correct	Passed	Failed	Prerequisite
1.20 Motor Imitation Phase					
1.21 Specific Motor Imitation Present randomly. Points to: Object on Table, Eyes, Nose, Ears, Light Extends Hands, Taps Teeth, Stands Up, Sits Down, Hands on Head	9/10				
2.00 VERBAL SECTION—RECEPTIVE					
2.10 Basic Receptive Phase					
2.11 Pointing to Body Parts Named	11/12			A	

126

Ear Eye Hair Hand Nose Teeth
___ ___ ___   ___   ___   ___
___ ___ ___   ___   ___   ___

2.12 Pointing to Objects Named

Baby Ball Bell Car Comb Hat Keys Shoe
___   ___   ___   ___ ___   ___ ___   ___
___   ___   ___   ___ ___   ___ ___   ___

14/16   B

2.12a Finding Concealed Objects Named: One Box
Same objects as 2.12

___ ___ ___ ___ ___ ___ ___ ___
___ ___ ___ ___ ___ ___ ___ ___

14/16   C   B

2.13 Pointing to Room Parts Named

Box Chair Door Floor Light Table
___ ___   ___   ___   ___   ___
___ ___   ___   ___   ___   ___

11/12   D

2.20 Receptive Expansion Phase I
Criterion = 2 of 4 parts

E

	Prerequisite	Failed	Passed	Number Correct	Criterion
2.21 Performance of Action Named: Body Parts	A	F			20/26
2.22 Performance of Action Named: Objects	B	G			14/18

2.21 Performance of Action Named: Body Parts

Wash ears	Wash hands	Wash face	Brush teeth	Brush hair	Comb hair
—	—	—	—	—	—

Wipe nose	Wipe mouth	Close eyes	Open eyes	Fold hands	Stand up	Sit down
—	—	—	—	—	—	—

2.22 Performance of Action Named: Objects

Push car	Rock baby	Throw ball	Ring bell	Shine shoe	Put on hat
—	—	—	—	—	—

Take off hat	Put on shoe	Take off shoe
—	—	—

2.22a Finding Concealed Objects Named: Two Boxes

Baby   Ball   Bell   Car   Shoe   Hat

___ ___ ___ ___ ___ ___

B
C
G

14/16

2.23 Performance of Action Named: Room Parts

Put key on chair	Put baby on chair	Open door	Close door	Mop floor
___	___	___	___	___
Sweep floor	Turn off light	Turn on light	Wash table	Put comb in box
___	___	___	___	___

D

16/20

2.30 Receptive Expansion Phase II
Criterion = 3 of 5 parts

H

2.31 Discriminating Possession: Body Parts

Show me the baby's _____ (or)

Show me Tommy's _____ .

A
F

14/16

Continued on next page.

Ears Eyes Face Hair Hands
Baby's —   —   —   —   —
Your —   —   —   —   —

Mouth Nose Teeth
Baby's —   —   —
Your —   —   —

	Criterion	Number Correct	Passed	Failed	Prerequisite
	11/12				B D G

2.32 Placing Objects in Prepositional Relationship to Room Parts

Put the _____ (choose from: baby, ball, bell, car, comb, hat, key, shoe)

	in box	on chair	under chair	on floor	under table	on table
	—	—	—	—	—	—

130

2.33	Giving Related Object Pairs				I	B

2.33 Giving Related Object Pairs
Give me the _____ and the _____.

shoe/sock	coat/hat	brush/comb
___	___	___

5/6   I   B

2.33a Finding Concealed Object Pairs: Toy Box Search
Same objects as 2.33

___	___	___

5/6   B C G I

2.34 Sorting Colors

Red	Green	Blue	Yellow	Black
___	___	___	___	___
White	Purple	Orange	Brown	
___	___	___	___	

7 correct 2 trials

2.40 Receptive Expansion Phase III
Criterion = 3 of 5 parts   J

		Criterion	Number Correct	Passed	Failed	Prerequisite
2.41	**Verb + Adverbial Place-Where Commands: Body/Space Awareness**					E
	Get in box — Look up — Look down — Fall down — Stand up — Turn round and round —	23/26				
	Walk on line — Walk around circle — Get in circle — Crawl under table —					
	Run to wall — Come to me — Crawl through tunnel —					
2.42	**Vocabulary Expansion: Nouns**		Record No. Correct			E
	Bread — Candy — Circle — Cup — Feet — Fork — Hammer —					
	Knees — Knife — Line — Wall — Nail — Napkin — Paper —					

Pencil Plate Soap Spoon Towel Tunnel Water
— — — — — — —

2.42a Finding Objects Named: Toy Box Search
If 90% correct on this part, go to 2.61a.

Baby Bell Ball Brush Car Coat Comb
— — — — — — —
Hat Keys Shoe Sock
— — — —

20/22

L   B C E G

2.43 Sorting Big/Little
Use 20 objects which are the same, except for size (10 big, 10 little).

Criterion: two correct sorts

Big Little Big Little
— — — —

4/4

133

	Criterion	Number Correct	Passed	Failed	Prerequisite
2.44 Pointing to Color Named Red　Green　Blue　Yellow　Black —　　—　　—　　—　　— White　Purple　Orange　Brown —　　—　　—　　　—	2/9 for two succes- sive days			M	
2.50 Receptive Expansion Phase IV Criterion = 3 of 5 parts				K	
2.51 Verb + Noun + Adverbial Place-Where Commands: Ball *Throw ball*　*Throw ball*　*Roll ball* *in box*　　　*up*　　　*through tunnel* —　　　　—　　　　— *Throw ball*　*Throw ball*　*Put ball* *at wall*　　　*to me*　　　*in circle* —　　　　—　　　　—	12/14			H	

134

2.52 Verb + Noun Commands: New Nouns

Hammer nail	Tear paper	Cut bread	Pour water	Make circle	Make line
—	—	—	—	—	—
Make tower	Ring bell	Push car	Rock baby		
—	—	—	—		

18/20 H

2.53 Pointing to Big One
Big and little pairs, one pair at a time (Show me the big one.)

Doll	Ball	Shoe	Car	Comb
—	—	—	—	—
Hat	Spoon	Sock	Nail	Box
—	—	—	—	—

18/20 N H

2.54 Give Me 1-5

One	Two	Three	Four	Five
—	—	—	—	—

9/10

	Criterion	Number Correct	Passed	Failed	Prerequisite
2.55 Pointing to Color + Object Named Use colors mastered in 2.44 and at least five of these objects: block, pencil, line, circle, ball, car, comb, shoe, sock, paper, cup. Fill in the blank with color and object. ___ ___ ___ ___ ___ ___ ___ ___ ___ ___ ___ ___	9/10				B G M H
2.60 Receptive Expansion Phase V					
2.61 Vocabulary Expansion: Nouns continued Not tested: refer to score on 2.42	38/42				

2.61a **Finding Object Named: Toy Box Search** Items = Five correct items from 2.42 Score = Score on the five items below plus the score from 2.42a. __ __ __ __ __ __ __ __ __ __				28/32	B C G J K L
2.62 **Pointing to Big/Little One** Use big/little pairs of 5 different objects, one pair at a time. __ __ __ __ __ Big Ltl Big Ltl Big Ltl Big Ltl Big Ltl				18/20	B G J K N
2.63 **Pointing to 1-5 + Object** Place 3 cards before the child: One with correct object, wrong number. One with correct number, wrong object. One with correct number and object. *Give me* ___(two)___ ___(keys)___ . (etc.) number object(s) Continued on next page.				9/10	B G J K

137

	Criterion	Number Correct	Passed	Failed	Prerequisite

3.00 VERBAL SECTION–EXPRESSIVE

3.10 Vocal Imitation Phase
Do this; say _____.

Ear	Eye	Hair	Hand	Nose	Teeth	Baby
Ball	Bell	Car	Comb	Hat	Keys	Shoe
Box	Chair	Door	Floor	Light	Table	

Criterion 20/40

Back-up Steps

Vowel Imitation: ah /a/ _____
                  ee /i/ _____
                  oo /u/ _____

Gross Vocal Imitation: Responds to "ah" with nonspecific
                       vocalization _____

Chaining to motor imitation: _____

3.20 Basic Expressive Phase

3.21 Naming Body Parts

Ear	Eye	Hair	Hand	Nose	Teeth
—	—	—	—	—	—
—	—	—	—	—	—

11/12

0

3.22 Naming Objects

Baby	Ball	Bell	Car	Comb	Hat
—	—	—	—	—	—
Keys	Shoe				
—	—				

14/16

P

10/20

139

Item	Task	Criterion	Number Correct	Passed	Failed	Prerequisite
3.22a	Naming Concealed Objects Same objects as 3.22 ___ ___ ___ ___ ___ ___	14/16			Q	P
3.23	Naming Room Parts Box Chair Door Floor Light Table ___ ___ ___ ___ ___ ___	11/12			R	
3.30	Expressive Expansion Phase I Criterion = 3 of 5 parts				S	
3.31	Discriminating Possession: Whose? with Body Parts Ear Eyes Hair Hands Nose Teeth *Baby's* ___ ___ ___ ___ ___ *Mine* ___ ___ ___ ___ ___	11/12				O

3.32 Naming Objects in Prepositional Relationship to Room Parts

Any match, such as *What is on the floor? Baby.*

Choose from: Baby, Ball, Bell, Car, Comb, Hat, Keys, Shoe

		P
In box	————	
On chair	————	14/16
On floor	————	T
On table	————	

3.32a Naming Missing Object: What's Gone?

Baby	Ball	Bell	Car	Comb	Hat	
——	——	——	——	——	——	14/16
Key	Shoe					P
——	——					Q
						T

3.33 Naming Room Part in Prepositional Relationship to Object

Response: One-word room part

Where is the _____ ? baby, ball, bell, car, comb, hat,
   key, shoe

	R
	11/12

Continued on next page.

		(In) box	(On) floor	(Under) chair
		___	___	___
		(On) chair	(On) table	(Under) table
		___	___	___

	Criterion	Number Correct	Passed	Failed	Prerequisite
3.34 Manding Actions: Verb-Noun Throw ___ Push ___	4/4			U	
3.40 Expressive Expansion Phase II Criterion = 3 of 5 parts				V	
3.41 Naming Colors Red Blue Green Yellow Black ___ ___ ___ ___ ___ Orange Purple Brown White ___ ___ ___ ___	4/18 Two colors both trials			W	S

142

3.41a Naming Concealed Colors Use colors correct on 3.41. — — — — — — — — — —			90% of colors mastered			S W Q
3.42 Naming Two Objects Baby-Socks Ball-Shoe Bell-Key Brush-Car ___ ___ ___ ___ Comb-Hat Coat-Ball ___ ___			11/12			P S
3.43 Naming Object + Room Part in Prepositional Relationship Response: Two words *Where is the* _____? baby, ball, bell, car, comb, hat, keys, shoe Baby ___ Ball ___ Bell ___ Comb ___ Floor Box Chair Table Car ___ Hat ___ Key ___ Shoe ___ Box Floor Chair Table			14/16			P R S T

		Criterion	Number Correct	Passed	Failed	Prerequisite
3.44	Counting to Five	2 correct trials			X	
	1 - 2 - 3 - 4 - 5					
	1 - 2 - 3 - 4 - 5					
3.50	Expressive Expansion Phase III					O P R S
3.51	Vocabulary Expansion: Naming Nouns *new nouns	80/90				

Ears Eyes Face* Hair Feet* Hands Knees*
___   ___   ___   ___   ___   ___   ___

Nose Mouth* Teeth Box Chair Door Wall*
___   ___   ___   ___ ___   ___   ___

Floor Light Table Hat Coat* Shoe Socks*
___   ___   ___   ___ ___   ___   ___

Spoon Plate Cup Fork* Napkin* Line*
___   ___   ___ ___   ___   ___

144

Circle* Tunnel* Baby Ball Block* Bell
__ __ __ __ __ __
Car Bread* Candy* Water* Comb Brush*
__ __ __ __ __ __
Towel* Soap* Nail* Hammer* Paper* Keys Pencil
__ __ __ __ __ __ __

P
Q
S

3.51a Vocabulary Expansion: What's Gone? with Three Objects

Items mastered in 3.51

Remove one item of a group of three.

Write the item tested in the (_____).

( ) ( ) ( ) ( ) ( ) ( )   ( ) ( ) ( ) ( ) ( ) ( )

( ) ( ) ( ) ( ) ( ) ( )   ( ) ( ) ( ) ( ) ( ) ( )

90% of items tested

Continued on next page.

145

	Criterion	Number Correct	Passed	Failed	Prerequisite

3.52 Manding Action: Verb + Noun with New Nouns
Response: Two words

Throw	Push	Hammer	Tear	Make	Ring	Rock
ball	car	nail	paper	tower	bell	baby
___	___	___	___	___	___	___
(___)	(___)	(___)	(___)	(___)	(___)	(___)

Criterion: 12/14   Prerequisite: U, V

3.53 Naming Color + Object
Use colors mastered in 3.41 and objects mastered in 3.22

___	___	___
___	___	___

Criterion: 9/10   Prerequisite: P, V, W

3.54 Counting Disappearing Objects 1-5
As tokens are placed in bank

1 - 2 - 3 - 4 - 5 _____
1 - 2 - 3 - 4 - 5 _____

Criterion: 2/2   Prerequisite: V, X

six

Sign Language and Total Communication

by Martha Snell*

Many retarded persons are frustrated by an inability to verbally communicate their needs, desires and thoughts; and the frustration is frequently heightened because their expressive skills are very low or non-existent even though they may have a high level of receptive or understanding skills. Since the problem is often simply the result of hearing loss which may be partially or fully corrected, hearing tests should always be a first step in developing a language program for non-verbal or low-verbal children.

Some retarded children with normal levels of hearing plateau during language training at an early level of sound imitation. They seem unable to produce or to perfect any understandable words although they may produce some sounds. For them a manual mode of expression can be taught along with continued training towards vocal expression. Manual expressive

* Martha Snell received her Ph.D. from Michigan State University in 1973 in Special Education. Her major interests are in the education of low-functioning retarded persons and in teacher training. Dr. Snell is currently on the faculty of the University of Virginia Special Education Department at Charlottesville. The author extends appreciation to Vivian Stevenson, M.S., Assistant Professor, Department of Elementary Education at Michigan State University, for her continued guidance in the writing of this chapter.

training provides the retarded non-verbal child with two remedies:

1. A temporary expressive communication system which would act to reduce social retardation by encouraging communication with peers and adults.

2. Cognitive expansion of receptive skills, laying the foundation for later vocal expression.

There is some support in the literature on deaf education to indicate that the early use of manual communication does not retard the development of meaningful vocalizations but does contribute to a higher cognitive level of stored information and understanding. Indications are that imitative sign training serves to facilitate receptive language skills in retarded hearing children with severe language handicaps.

The signs and training procedures described here have been used in language training programs with a small number of hearing and hearing impaired retarded children who had severe language retardation, little or no vocal expression, and receptive skills that varied from none to mastery of the first Receptive Expansion Phase. When training the expansion phases not directly discussed in this chapter, the trainer will probably need to expand the sign glossary by referring to the materials cited at the end of this chapter, and to generalize the principles of learning and manual communication instruction.

Manual signing may be used in the following cases:

1. Deaf children.

2. Children who are receiving vocal imitation training and who have some receptive skills and possibly some spontaneous manual expression, but no understandable vocal expressive skills.

3. All children who have little or no receptive, vocal expressive, vocal imitative, motor imitative or even attending skills as measured by the I-I.

The mode of manual communication is Sign Language coupled with the procedure of total communication;

it is the simultaneous presentation of visual-manual language with oral spoken English. The signs are part of the American Sign Language (Ameslan). Sign Language is a less complex mode of manual communication and differentiated from other modes such as Signed English, the Simultaneous Method, Finger Spelling and Manual English because, generally, there is not a one-to-one correspondence between Sign Language and spoken English. Some words in Sign Language, such as articles and morphemes, are not signed; Sign Language does not have a morpheme-by-morpheme equivalence to English. In the present application of Sign Language, however, one aspect of Signed English is incorporated to provide manual language with syntax closer to spoken English: the verb "to be" is signed by the trainer during the receptive and expressive phases.

The child, who may or may not have normal hearing acuity, is taught to understand and to use signs which communicate simple words and concepts. The trainer uses signs to communicate simple words and concepts, simple commands, words for objects, body parts, activities, etc., while simultaneously speaking. The practice of total communication allows the hearing learner to associate signs auditorily with spoken words and concepts. While the hearing impaired learner may make some auditory association, depending upon his residual hearing, he will learn primarily a visual association between meaningful signs and the mouth and facial movements of spoken English. This latter association is an important early step in speech reading.

GENERAL SUGGESTIONS FOR SIGNING

1. Learn signs thoroughly before beginning to train in order to be consistent and smooth in the rhythm of presenting each sign at a slow, deliberate pace.

2. Signs must be positioned correctly in order not to confuse one sign with another visually.

3. Signs should be placed as close to the body as possible and positioned below the shoulder, but above the waist, except for those signs which must be made near the face.

4. Directly face the person with whom you are manually communicating, keeping the mouth and hands within the child's visual range. If there are visual handicaps, the trainer must adjust signing distance accordingly.

5. Teach standardized signs in order to encourage generalization to other situations and persons, to make learning easier, and to eliminate the confusion that would result if more than one sign were used for the same object, person, action or concept.

INITIAL PROCEDURES FOR INSTRUCTION OF NEW SIGNS

1. Emphasize the signs by slowing the pace and by increasing their size enough to be seen clearly by the child. For example, the standard sign for "come" (index fingers rotated over each other in circles and moved towards the body) can be enlarged so that a wide circle is made with the hands which is begun a distance out from the chest and then brought towards the body.

2. Repeat signs, especially those that cannot be made larger (e.g., nose).

3. Give the sign slowly to increase the chances that a child will see and eventually understand it.

4. Maintain eye contact with the child and keep facial expressions and "body language" consistent with what is spoken and signed.

5. Acknowledge the child's own signs (if he has them) for words being taught, but reinforce only the standardized signs selected for instruction.

MANUAL VOCAL STIMULATION

Regardless of whether the child has normal or impaired hearing, the trainer always speaks in a clear, firm voice while signing. This practice is very important so that children without hearing or with limited hearing eventually will learn to speech read; and those with hearing and the ability to understand some spoken words will continue to use and expand those oral skills. Also, whenever possible, the trainer pairs each sign with vocal expression so that the child can begin to associate the spoken word with the manual sign for that word; the rate of speaking and signing should be matched.

ATTENDING PHASE

The typical training sequence for this phase is illustrated in Figure 7 (page 175). Trial 1 illustrates specifically what the trainer does when training 1.13 Looking at Objects. The trainer points to an object on the table while signing and says *Look at this;* when the child looks, he is praised: the trainer signs and says *Good.* If the child is on a token reinforcement system, he is given a token. Trials 2a and 2b illustrate the procedure to follow if a child does not perform the expected behavior (stimulus presentation repeated, physical prompt given to assist the correct attending behavior, followed by signed and spoken praise). In trial 2c the physical prompt is faded out as quickly as possible over the following trials; the expectation is that the child will eventually attend appropriately without assistance. During this phase the child will learn only the meaning of the signs and words in the commands and is not expected to use them expressively. For the inattentive child who must have the commands repeated the sign for "now" may be added to the command *Look at this* **now.**

Since signs do not always have single interpretations, and because Sign Language does not translate English word for word, the guide below should be used to match signs with spoken commands for each part in the Attending Phase. Note that the sign for "attend" rather than for "look" is used by the trainer in 1.14 Pre-Trial Eye Contact and is spoken as *Watch me.* This sign is clearer in its meaning, and the word "watch" is clearer than "attend."

Part	Words Spoken by Trainer	Words Signed by Trainer
	A. Prompting a response:	
1.11	*Sit,* or *You sit.*	Sit, or You sit.
1.12	*Be still.*	Still.
	B. Training a response:	
1.12	*Sit still.*	Sit still.
1.13	*Look at this.*	Look this.
1.14	*Watch me; look at this.*	Watch me; look this.

SIGNS FOR THE ATTENDING PHASE

Whenever specific handshapes of the manual alphabet are included as part of a sign description, refer to the Manual Alphabet (Figure 11, p. 180) at the end of this chapter. In addition, signs for praising a child are found in the Glossary of Manual Signs, p. 185.

1. **Sit/Chair**
   Both the index and middle fingers of the right hand are laid across the left index and middle fingers. The palms face downward.

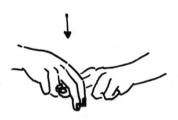

2. **Still/Quiet/Be Quiet**
   Index finger of the right hand held flat is placed against the lips with the other hand held flat just below; both hands are then swept downward to a position parallel to the floor.

3. Now
Bend both hands with palms facing up in front of you, waist high; move hands slightly downward.

4. Attend/Watch
(Say *Watch* when signing.) Hold hand with palms facing each other like blinders next to each eye; move hands forward and down.

5. Look
Hold the "V" handshape so that fingertips almost touch the eyes; rotate the hand so the fingertips move and point straight ahead.

6. Me
Point towards yourself with the right index finger.

7. This/These

With right index finger pointing to the left open palm, move it in a circular motion before touching palm of left hand.

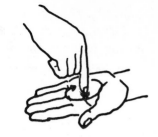

8. You (singular)

Point straight at the other person with the right index finger.

MOTOR IMITATION PHASE

A sample training sequence for this phase is illustrated in Figure 8, page 176. Again, as in other phases, if the child does not correctly imitate the task modeled by the trainer or does not give a successively better approximation, physical prompts are given after a repetition of the stimulus presentation. Prompts are quickly faded. These procedures are illustrated in trials 2a, b, and c.

During this phase, rather than saying and signing *Do this* (as in 1.20), another command, clearer in its signs, is substituted. The trainer signs and says *Watch and you do* instead. The child learns the skill of motor imitation by understanding the signs and words for the command *Watch and you do*.

The child learns and practices motor imitation skills in this phase. Such practice is vital since imitative prompting relies upon the child's ability to copy specific signs. During expressive phases this type of prompt is used repeatedly in teaching the use of new signs.

Additional imitative training begins with gross hand and arm movements and progresses to finer hand and finger movements, finger plays,* and specific signs. For example, in this latter stage of training the trainer first says and signs the imitative command *Watch and do this,* and then presents a meaningful sign for a word (e.g., *hair*: takes hold of a piece of hair with forefinger and thumb) and at the same time vocalizes the word. The vocalization is used to begin an association of arm, hand, and finger movements with mouth movement and sound. The auditory understanding of the spoken words for the hearing student and the visual understanding for the non-hearing child is learned during the receptive phases.

SIGNS FOR THE MOTOR IMITATION PHASE

9. **Attend/Watch**
   (Say *Watch* when signing.) Hold hands with palms facing each other like blinders next to each eye; move hands forward and down.

10. **And**
    Hold the right hand with fingers spread so palm faces you and fingertips point left; move the hand right bringing fingertips together.

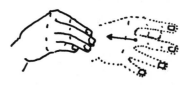

---

* For finger play games refer to L. B. Scott, *Rhymes for fingers and flannelboards* (St. Louis: Webster Publishing Co., 1960).

11. You (singular)
Point straight at the other person with the right index finger.

12. Do/Activity
Hold both hands in the "C" position with palms down, and move both hands to the left and right a few times holding the "C" position.

VOCAL IMITATION PHASE

During this phase the child is taught to imitate gross sounds, vowels, words, and phrases. The child does not learn to use signs but only to receptively understand the signs for the command *Say.* However, for the child in the Sign Language program extensive work in this phase is necessary in order eventually to develop speech, if at all possible, which will replace the signs.

The two commands that are spoken and signed in this phase are listed in the table below. The single words and phrases are also spoken and signed for imitation. While the trainer emphasizes the word or words to be imitated, the signs for these are also emphasized. The "ah" sound and the other vowel sounds for gross vocal and vowel imitation are not signed, but only spoken.

Part	Words Spoken by Trainer	Words Signed by Trainer
Gross Vocal Imitation	*Watch and you do; say, AH.*	Watch and you do; say _____.
Vowel Imitation	*Say, OH.*	Say _____ .
Word Imitation	*Say, baby.*	Say, baby.
Phrase Imitation	*Say, baby's nose.*	Say, baby nose.

Vocal imitation is generally more difficult than motor imitation. First, unlike motor imitation where it is possible to prompt a child physically, vocal imitation cannot be easily prompted. Second, the act of producing a sound is not as obvious as are motor acts (e.g., moving objects or body parts). Third, differences between sounds are even more difficult to discriminate aurally and visually and to reproduce. When there is any impairment in hearing, these latter difficulties are magnified. For these reasons a number of training techniques are suggested to elicit vocal imitation. The trainer should change techniques if after sufficient time a particular technique does not evoke sound imitation.

Stimulating a child to make a gross imitation after the trainer says *Ah*, first necessitates using the child's skills in motor imitation with body parts, gradually having him imitate tasks which bring him closer and closer to producing the sound. The trainer presents some imitative tasks involving large body movements (e.g., hit the table, extend arms horizontally at sides) proceeding next to finer imitative tasks (e.g., raise hands, pat head) and then progressing to those tasks which involve the face (touch nose, open mouth, etc.). Finally, a vocalization task is presented. The child is given in sign and words the same command *Watch and you do* to cue him to make another imitative response, followed by the vocal command *Say, Ah.* **Any sound response by the child is regarded as a gross vocal imitation and is reinforced.**

At times a child will be able to imitate movements of the mouth perfectly, but still be unable to produce a sound in imitation. A number of methods can be tried with these children to increase their discrimination of the sound itself. A small metal can (like a one-pound coffee can) is held to the mouth by the trainer when giving the "Ah" sound in the command *Watch and you do; say, ah.* The sound is amplified by echoing in the can. The can is handed to the child who may try and fail several times before making a sound into it. The trainer should praise the child's attempts to imitate; repeat the command, and show the child again. A long paper tube, like a paper towel tube, is used in a similar way to produce novel sounds that a child may be more likely to imitate. An auditory trainer device can also be used to increase the volume and clarity of the sounds. In a similar way the trainer signs the command voicing the vocal model "ah" into the auditory device, which is then passed to the child.

Another technique involves teaching a series of imitative motor movements which end with a sound (i.e., hitting table, standing up, putting hands to mouth, and then making a noise). This technique attempts to develop an imitative chain (training the first task, then adding the second task to the first, etc.) and to append a sound onto the end of the chain of behaviors.

If the child is at times making sound without the command to do so, other teaching techniques are available. The trainer reinforces the child only when he produces sounds. This procedure merely serves to increase the number of sounds the child makes during training sessions and increases the likelihood that he will make sounds when the command to imitate is introduced. The trainer then imitates the child's sounds as he is vocalizing. Using these same sounds, the trainer attempts to take the lead, getting the child to repeat the sound after his presentation. Reinforcement is given immediately following any vocalization that occurs after the trainer's presentation. Next the command *Say* _____ is introduced with the same sound. Later the trainer varies the rhythm of the same sound and the sounds themselves, gradually expecting the child to imitate vowels and words.

SIGNS FOR THE VOCAL IMITATION PHASE
Refer to motor imitation signs for: 9. Watch, 10. And, 11. You, 12. Do.

13. **Say**
    Hold the right index finger parallel to the mouth; circle it forward and down.

BASIC RECEPTIVE AND
RECEPTIVE EXPANSION PHASES
The signs are given at the same rate as the spoken command (*Show me the ball, Show me the baby's nose, Go get the comb,* etc.). When the key words are emphasized orally, the signs for those words are emphasized also (e.g., objects, room parts, body parts, activities, etc.). However, the other signs in each command sentence also are given as illustrated below. The articles (a, an, the) and the plural and the possessive "s" are not signed. But the conjunction (and), the prepositions (in, on), verbs, nouns and pronouns are signed. Again, the child may not learn to use the signs expressively in this phase, but he will learn the meaning of the words and signs that he will later use in the expressive phases.

Part	Words Spoken by Trainer	Words Signed by Trainer
2.11	*Show me Tommy's nose.*	Show me Tommy nose.
2.12	*Show me the keys.*	Show me key.
2.13	*Show me the box.*	Show me box.

As in the other phases, a child is praised for successful responses and successively better approximations; this is illustrated in trial 1 of Figure 9, page 177. In addition, after a correct response, verbal feedback is given by the trainer. Verbal feedback includes signing and saying the response just performed by the child; e.g., *That is the hat.* Note that verb contractions are avoided in this sign language program so that signs and words can be given simultaneously.

When errors or no responses are made during the learning period, a variety of prompts can be given. And when using imitative prompts, the trainer models the correct response which is then imitated by the child; this is illustrated in trials 2a, b, and c. A cuing prompt includes pointing to or tapping near the correct choice as well as highlighting that choice with redundancy cues (e.g., red paper under the correct choice). Finally a physical prompt can be used in which the child is assisted in making the correct motor response (e.g., trainer lifts child's hand and places it on the correct choice). Again, prompts should be faded out within a short time.

SIGNS FOR THE RECEPTIVE PHASES

All the signs for the Basic Receptive Phase are listed below. However, there is only a partial listing of signs from the Receptive Expansion Phases. The references listed at the end of this chapter are good sources for the remaining signs.

When signing the child's name, as in 2.11 Pointing to Body Parts, the trainer decides upon a particular sign to stand for that child's name. Generally the first letter of the child's name is signed in a fixed position or with a motion that relates to a physical characteristic of that child. For example, Jill who has long hair could be signed with the letter "J" in a position near the top of the head and which is then moved down in front of the shoulder. The Manual Alphabet from which these letter signs are taken appears as Figure 11, p. 180.

Not all signs for this phase are listed below. For other signs and their reference numbers check the Glossary of Manual Signs, p. 185.

14. Show/Demonstrate
Hold the right index finger-tip in the open palm of the left hand, palm out, finger-tips up; move both hands forward in this position.

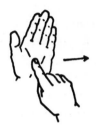

15. Ears
Point to your ear with right index finger.

16. Eyes
Point to your eye with right index finger.

17. Face
Draw a circle in front of the face with the right index finger.

18. Hair
Hold onto a piece of hair with thumb and index finger.

19. Hands
Using small finger edge of open right hand, slash across top of left wrist; repeat motion using left hand to mark off right wrist.

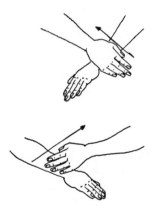

20. Mouth
Point to mouth with index finger.

21. Nose
Point to or touch your nose with right index finger.

22. Teeth
Open lips and point to your teeth.

23. Baby
Rest the right hand and arm on the left arm so as to pantomine rocking a baby.

24. **Ball**
Hold hands cupped together, one palm facing down, the other up; exchange positions quickly.

25. **Bell**
Move a relaxed "O" handshape back and forth, as though ringing a small bell.

26. **Car**
Using both fists, reach out as if holding a steering wheel; move hands in a semicircle.

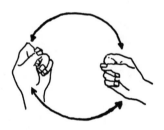

27. **Comb**
Move spread fingers downward through hair.

28. Hat
Pat top of head several times with right open palm.

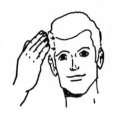

29. Key
Bend the right index finger; place the knuckle into the open palm of the left hand and twist as if turning a key.

30. Shoes
Hold both fists in the "S" handshape; strike fists together several times.

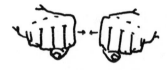

31. Go
Hold the index fingers parallel and facing yourself; move them around each other and away from yourself.

32. Get
Hold open hands, the right above and to the right of the left hand and facing each other; close into fists, the right on top of the left.

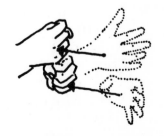

33. Box

Hold both hands facing each other in front of you; move one on top of the other as if forming the sides, top and bottom of a box.

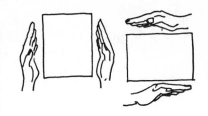

34. Sit/Chair

Both the index and middle fingers of the right hand are laid across the left index and middle fingers. The palms face downward.

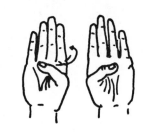

35. Door

Hold both hands in the "B" handshape with palms facing outward and sides of index fingers together; as if a door, swing right palm back and forth at the index finger.

36. Floor

Hold both hands open and apart facing the floor; bring them together.

37. Light (which is switched on and off)

Hold right hand in the "And" position (see No. 10) and move forward opening hand with fingers spread.

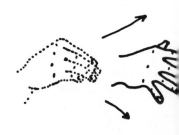

38. Table
   Hold hands together with palms facing out and fingers perpendicular to palms; move hands apart to outline a table top and drop hands down flattened and facing each other.

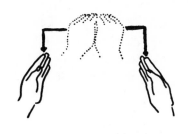

39. Your/Yours
   Face palm out; move it away from body.

40. Put/Move
   Hold the hands down in front of you in the open "And" position (see No. 10); move and lift them to the right while bringing the fingers together.

41. On
   Place open palm of right hand on back of left hand keeping both palms face down.

42. In
   Hold right fingertips together and place into cup formed by left hand.

43. Under/Below/Beneath
Hold both hands flat and open, palms down, with right hand under left; rotate right hand counterclockwise.

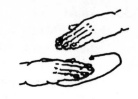

44. Give
Both hands are held facing downward in the "And" position (see No. 10); hands are brought palm up in toward the body and extended out flat as if giving something to another.

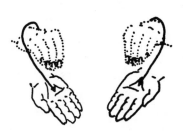

BASIC EXPRESSIVE AND EXPRESSIVE EXPANSION PHASES

The child learns to sign during the expressive phases. He is taught to answer various questions with one-sign responses, using the signs for objects, room parts, body parts, and activities. After the child learns one-sign responses he is taught to combine signs into two- and three-sign responses (e.g., *my nose, ball on chair*).

Figure 10 illustrates some primary training procedures used during the Basic Expressive Phase which are generalized to the other expressive phases. When a child correctly signs the name of an object (room part, body part, etc.) or approximates that sign during early training, as illustrated in trials 1 and 2 respectively, the trainer reinforces him in words and signs with praise and verbal feedback. However, when a child approximates the sign for an object (room part, etc.) at a level inferior to his expected performance, the trainer should repeat the stimulus presentation, as in trial 3b, and provide an imitative prompt, thereby stimulating the child to the correct response. This imitative prompt should be quickly faded out; reinforce the child during later trials for correct responses made without prompts.

When a child incorrectly signs another object (room part, etc.), the trainer ignores it, or nonpunitively informs him of his error by ignoring the response for 30 seconds as in trial 4a (Figure 10). He then repeats the stimulus presentation and immediately provides an imitative prompt in order to prevent another error. During later trials this prompt should be faded out. If the child does not respond to the stimulus presentation, as in trial 5a, the trainer repeats the stimulus and provides imitative prompting. In this most difficult learning situation, when no response is made by the child, physical prompts also are given by moving the child's hands in the correct pattern. Again a fading procedure follows; the physical prompts are faded first, followed by the elimination of the imitative prompts. **Avoid using negative language, such as** *No,* **as it connotes failure.**

When new signs are especially difficult for a child, additional training may be given in the Motor Imitation Phase to allow practice in copying specific hand and finger movements without the requirement to associate them meaningfully to words. During these training sessions the trainer will sign and say the command *Watch and you do;* no objects need be presented.

Because the Ameslan system does not sign English word for word, the commands spoken and those signed are listed below for some of the expressive parts. As mentioned earlier, the signs for "is" and "are," although not generally used with Sign Language, are included for optional use to more closely approximate English.

It is especially important when a child reaches this expressive level of training that the adults in his environment encourage and reinforce any effort to use signs. Pictures of the signs should be posted in visible areas of the school, ward or home, and all adults in the environment should become familiar with those signs, and use every opportunity to reinforce the child in expressive and receptive attempts to communicate.

Part	Words Spoken by Trainer	Words Signed by Trainer
3.21 3.51	*What is this?*	What (is) this?
3.22	*What is this?*	What (is) this?
3.22a 3.42	*What is in the box?*	What (is) in box?
3.23	*What is this? (or that)*	What (is) this? (or that)
3.31	*Whose nose is this?*	Whose nose?
3.32	*What is on the table? (or in)*	What (is) on table? (or in)
3.32a 3.51a	*What is gone?*	What disappeared?
3.33 3.43	*Where is the hat?*	Where (is) hat?

SIGNS FOR THE EXPRESSIVE PHASES

Not all signs for this phase are listed below. For other signs and their reference number, check the Glossary of Manual Signs, page 185.

45. What

Sweep right index finger down and over open left palm.

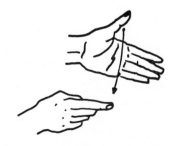

46. Is

Form the sign for the letter "I" in front of the mouth; move it away from the mouth.

47. Are

Form the sign for the letter "R" in front of the mouth; move it forward from the mouth.

48. That/Those

Hold right-handed "Y" handshape over left extended palm; bring right hand down to the left.

49. Whose/Who/Whom

Draw a small circle around closed lips with right index finger.

50. My/Mine
Lay open palm on chest.

51. Disappear/Gone
Form the open "And" hands (No. 10) and hold with palm facing self; move hands out to the sides forming fists with the thumbs pointed upward.

52. Where
Hold both hands palm up and flat, and rotate in a circle each to the outside.

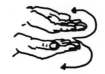

ADDITIONAL SIGNS

Other signs are used during language training to praise and to give the child corrective feedback. As mentioned earlier, the Manual Alphabet used by the deaf of North America (Figure 11) may be consulted for specific hand positions in some signs as well as for each child's name-sign.

53. Good
Hold right hand with fingers touching lips; move hand down and place it palm up onto open left palm.

54. Money/Tokens
Strike the back of the fingers of right hand onto open palm of left hand a few times.

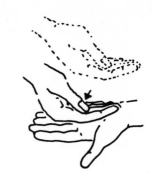

55. No
Place closed fingers of right hand across left with palms facing inwards; uncross hands and move out and downward.

56. Yes
Hold the "S" handshape with palm facing out; bend at the wrist and let fist drop.

Figure 7   Attending Phase Training Sequence

Trial	Trainer's Stimulus Presentation	Trainer's Prompt	Child's Response	Consequences Provided by Trainer	
				Reinforcing	Verbal Feedback
1	Point to object; sign and say *Look at this.*		Child looks.	Sign and say *Good.* Give token.	
2a	Point to object; sign and say *Look at this.*		Child makes no response.		
2b	Repeat.	Physical prompt: turn child's head and lift object.	Child looks.	Sign and say *Good.* Give token.	
2c	Repeat.	Fade out.	Child looks.	Sign and say *Good.* Give token.	

Figure 8   Motor Imitation Phase Training Sequence

Trial	Trainer's Stimulus Presentation	Trainer's Prompt	Child's Response	Consequences Provided by Trainer — Reinforcing	Verbal Feedback
1	Sign and say *Watch and you do* as imitative task is modeled (stand up).		Child imitates motor task (stands up).	Sign and say *Good.* Give token.	
2a	Sign and say *Watch and you do* as imitative task is modeled (stand up).		Child does not stand.		
2b	Repeat.	Physical prompt: take child's hands and pull him up.	Child stands.	Sign and say *Good.* Give token.	
2c	Repeat.	Fade out.	Child stands.	Sign and say *Good.* Give token.	

176

Figure 9   Basic Receptive Phase Training Sequence

Trial	Trainer's Stimulus Presentation	Trainer's Prompt	Child's Response	Consequences Provided by Trainer	
				Reinforcing	Verbal Feedback
1	Object(s) visible; trainer signs and says *Show me the* hat.		Child touches **hat**.	Sign and say *Good.* Give token.	Sign and say *That is the* **hat**.
2a	Trainer signs and says *Show me Billy's* **nose**.		Child touches ear.		
2b	Repeat.	Imitative prompt: trainer signs and says *Watch and you do,* then touches child's nose.	Child touches his **nose**.	Sign and say *Good.* Give token.	Sign and say *That is* **Billy's nose**.
2c	Repeat.	Fade out.	Child touches his **nose**.	Sign and say *Good.* Give token.	Sign and say *That is* **Billy's nose**.

Figure 10   Expansion Phase Training Sequence

Trial	Trainer's Stimulus Presentation	Trainer's Prompt	Child's Response	Consequences Provided by Trainer	
				Reinforcing	Verbal Feedback
1	Present the ball, sign and ask *What is this?*		Signs ball correctly.	Sign and say *Good.* Give token.	Sign and say *That is the ball.*
2	Present the key, sign and ask *What is this?*		Approximates sign for key (twisting motion with thumb and index finger).	Sign and say *Good.* Give token.	Sign and say *That is the key.*
3a	Present the key, sign and ask *What is this?*		Same.		
3b	Repeat	Imitative prompt: sign and say *Watch and you do*; key.	Signs key correctly.	Sign and say *Good.* Give token.	Sign and say *That is the key.*
4a	Present the shoe, sign and ask *What is this?*		Signs key.		

4b	Repeat. Immediately follow with imitative prompt.	Imitative prompt: sign and say *Watch and you do;* **shoe.**	Signs **shoe** correctly.	Sign and say *Good.* Give token.	Sign and say *That is the* **shoe.**
5a	Present the **hat**, sign and ask *What is this?*		No response.		
5b	Repeat.	Imitative prompt: sign and say *Watch and you do;* **hat.** Physical prompts: assist as needed.	Signs **hat** correctly.	Sign and say *Good.* Give token.	Sign and say *That is the* **shoe.**

Figure 11   Manual Alphabet

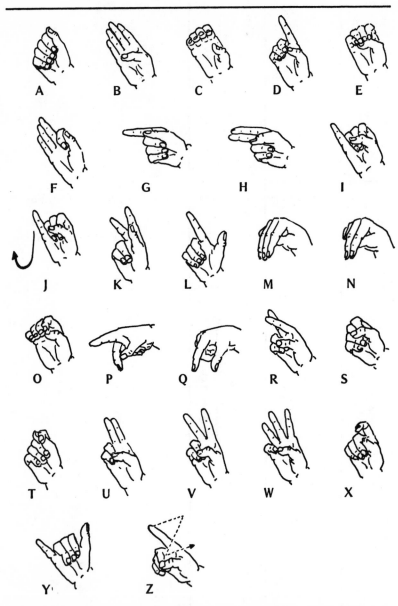

Appreciation is extended to the following publishers for their kind permission to use the material cited for adaptation.

Gospel Publishing House: L. L. Riekehof, *Talk to the deaf*. For signs and descriptions 7, 3-6, 8-17, 20, 21, 23, 26, 28-32, 34, 35, 39-45, 48-54, 56 and the Manual Alphabet.

National Association of the Deaf: T. J. O'Rourke, *A basic course in manual communication*. For signs and descriptions 1, 2, 6-8, 11, 13, 23, 26, 29, 32, 34, 38, 41, 42, 45, 46, 48-50, 53-56.

Pinecrest State School: M. Owens and B. Harper, *Sign Language: A teaching manual for cottage parents of non-verbal retardates*. For signs and descripti · 15, 16, 18, 20, 21, 24, 26-29.

Watson, D. O. *Talk with your hands* (Winnecone, Wisconsin). For signs and descriptions 33, 36, 37.

Signs and training suggestions have been taken from these sources:

Fant, L. J. Jr. *Ameslan, An introduction to American Sign Language.* Silver Spring, Md.: National Association of the Deaf, 1972.

Fant, L. J. Jr. *Say it with hands.* Silver Spring, Md.: National Association of the Deaf, 1964.

Hoemann, H. W. and Shirley, A. *Sign Language flash cards.* Silver Spring, Md.: National Association of the Deaf, 1973.

O'Rourke, T. J. *A basic course in manual communication.* Silver Spring, Md.: National Association of the Deaf, 1970.

Owens, M. and Harper, B. *Sign Language: A teaching manual for cottage parents of non-verbal retardates.* Pineville, La.: Department of Speech and Hearing, Pinecrest State School, 1971.

Riekehof, L. L. *Talk to the deaf.* Springfield, Mo.: Gospel Publishing House, 1963.

Watson, D. *Talk with your hands.* Winneconne, Wis., 1964.

References

Alterman, A. Language and the education of children with early profound deafness. *American Annals of the Deaf, 115,* 1970, 514-521.

Bricker, D. D Imitative sign training as a facilitator of word-object association with low-functioning children. *American Journal of Mental Deficiency, 76,* 1972, 509-516.

Hester, M.S. Manual communication. In P. V. Doctor (Ed.) *Proceedings of the Council on Education of the Deaf of the 41st Meeting of the Convention of American Instructors of the Deaf.* Gallaudet College, Washington, D.C., 1963.

Hoffman, B. E. An era of exploration. *American Annals of the Deaf, 115,* 1970, 55-56.

Meadow, K. P. Early manual communication in relation to the deaf child's intellectual, social, and communicative functioning. *American Annals of the Deaf, 113,* 1968, 9-41.

Quigley, S.P. *The influence of fingerspelling on the development of the language communication, and educational achievement in deaf children.* Urbana, Ill.: Institute for Research on Exceptional Children, University of Illinois, 1969.

Quigley, S. P. Language research in countries other than the United States. *Volta Review, 852,* 1966, 57-72.

Stevenson, E. A. A study of the educational achievement of deaf children of deaf parents. Berkeley: California School for the Deaf, 1964.

Stuckless, E. R. and Birch, J. W. The influence of early manual communication on the linguistic development of deaf children. *American Annals of the Deaf, 3,* 1966, 499-503.

Vernon, M., and Koh, S. D. Early manual communication and deaf children's achievement. *American Annals of the Deaf, 115,* 1970, 527-536.

Vernon, M. and Koh, S. D. Effects of oral preschool compared to early manual communication on education and communication in deaf children. *American Annals of the Deaf, 116,* 1971, 569-574.

For further reference to techniques for hearing assessment of non-verbal retarded children consult:

Berger, S. L. A clinical program for developing multimodal language responses with atypical deaf children. In McLean, J. E., Yoder, D. E., and Schiefelbusch, R. L. (Eds.) *Language intervention with the retarded: Developing strategies.* Baltimore: University Park Press, 1972.

Bricker, D., Bricker, W. A. and Larsen, L. A. *Operant audiometry manual for difficult-to-test children.* Nashville, Tennessee: Institute on Mental Retardation and Intellectual Development, Peabody College, IMRID papers and reports, *V* (19), 1968.

Fulton, R. T. A program of developmental research in audiologic procedures. In Schiefelbusch, R. L. (Ed.) *Language of the mentally retarded.* Baltimore: University Park Press, 1972, 169-188.

Lloyd, L. L. and Fulton, R. T. Audiology's contribution to communications programming with the retarded. In McLean, J. E., Yoder, D. E., and Schiefelbusch, R. L. (Eds.) *Language intervention with the retarded: Developing strategies.* Baltimore: University Park Press, 1972, 111-129.

Siegenthaler, B. M. and Haspiel, G., *T. I. P. D. I. P.* (Threshold by Identification of Pictures—Discrimination by Identification of Pictures). University Park, Pa.: The Pennsylvania State University, 1970.

GLOSSARY OF MANUAL SIGNS

activity/do, 12
and, 10
are, 47
attend/watch, 4, 9

baby, 23
ball, 24
bell, 25
below/beneath/under, 43
box, 33

car, 26
chair/sit, 1, 34
comb, 27

demonstrate/show, 14
disappear/gone, 51
do/activity, 12
door, 35

ears, 15
eyes, 16

face, 17
floor, 36

get, 32
give, 44
go, 31
gone/disappear, 51
good, 53

hair, 18
hands, 19
hat, 28

in, 42
is, 46

key, 29

light, 37
look, 5

me, 6
money/tokens, 54
mouth, 20
move/put, 40
my/mine, 50

name (of the child), see p.161
no, 55
nose, 21
now, 3

on, 41

put/move, 40

quiet/be quiet/still, 2

say, 13
shoes, 30
show/demonstrate, 14
sit/chair, 1, 34
still/quiet/be quiet, 2

table, 38
teeth, 22
that/those, 48
this/these, 7
tokens/money, 54

under/below/beneath, 43

watch/attend, 4, 9
what, 45
where, 52
whose/whom/who, 49

yes, 56
you, 8, 11
your/yours, 39